ADDICTIONS

Addictions

Maree Teesson, Louisa Degenhardt, & Wayne Hall

National Drug and Alcohol Research Centre
University of New South Wales – Sydney, Australia

First published 2002 by Psychology Press Ltd
27 Church Road, Hove, East Sussex, BN3 2FA, UK

www.psypress.co.uk

Simultaneously published in the USA and Canada
by Taylor & Francis Inc
29 West 35th Street, New York, NY 10001 USA

Reprinted 2003

Psychology Press is part of the Taylor & Francis Group

© 2002 Psychology Press

British Library Cataloguing in Publication Data
A catalogue record for this book is available from the British Library

Library of Congress Cataloging-in-Publication Data
A catalog record for this book is available from the Library of Congress

ISBN 1-84169-313-8 (Hbk)
ISBN 1-84169-314-6 (Pbk)
ISSN 1368-454X (Clinical Psychology: A Modular Course)

Cover design by Joyce Chester
Cover illustration by The University of New South Wales
Typeset in Palatino by Mayhew Typesetting, Rhayader, Powys
Printed and bound in the UK by TJ International Ltd, Padstow, Cornwall

Contents

Acknowledgements

We would like to acknowledge Heather Proudfoot for assistance with literature reviews, Dr Vaughan Rees for assistance with the cognitive behavioural intervention for cannabis dependence, Kate Hetherington for research assistance and editing, Andrew Baillie for discussion and thoughtful comments, and the staff of the National Drug and Alcohol Research Centre, University of New South Wales, Sydney, whose research is the cornerstone of this book.

Series preface

Clinical Psychology: A Modular Course was designed to overcome the problems faced by the traditional textbook in conveying what psychological disorders are really like. All the books in the series, written by leading scholars and practitioners in the field, can be read as stand-alone texts, but they will also integrate with the other modules to form a comprehensive resource in clinical psychology. Students of psychology, medicine, nursing, and social work, as well as busy practitioners in many professions, often need an accessible but thorough introduction to how people experience anxiety, depression, addiction, or other disorders, how common they are, and who is most likely to suffer from them, as well as up-to-date research evidence on the causes and available treatments. The series will appeal to those who want to go deeper into the subject than the traditional textbook will allow, and base their examination answers, research, projects, assignments, or practical decisions on a clearer and more rounded appreciation of the clinical and research evidence.

Chris R. Brewin

Other titles in this series:

Depression
Constance Hammen

Anxiety
S. Rachman

Childhood Disorders
Philip C. Kendall

Stress and Trauma
Patricia A. Resick

The nature of addiction 1

Many people will drink alcohol in their lifetime and a minority will use illicit drugs. Not all people will develop problems with alcohol and other drugs but some will and the extent of the problems they experience will differ from person to person. Consider the following scenario:

> Robin is a young male, who goes out on Friday and Saturday nights with his friends. Robin usually drinks a lot on these occasions, although he doesn't usually drink much during the rest of the week. On a regular night out Robin drinks around 20 drinks over a period of 8 hours until he is fully drunk. Robin's friends, while also drinking, do not drink as much as Robin. Robin's friends are concerned for Robin as he has been involved in a number of pub fights while drunk. He was recently involved in a brawl that resulted in his breaking a stranger's nose and Robin being arrested by the police.

As in this example, it is not just drinking alcohol that results in problems but the consequences of heavy alcohol use. A person is considered to have a problem with alcohol or other drugs when he or she has difficulty controlling their use (Robin drinks until he is fully intoxicated), when obtaining, using, and recovering from alcohol or drugs consumes a disproportionate amount of the individual's time, and the individual continues to drink alcohol or take drugs in the face of problems that the person knows to be caused by it (such as brawling in the pub). Individuals typically become tolerant to the effects of alcohol or drugs, requiring larger doses to achieve the desired psychological effect, and abrupt cessation of use often produces a withdrawal syndrome. Many experience other psychological and physical health problems, and their alcohol or drug use often adversely affects the lives of their spouses, children, and other family members, friends and workmates.

In summary, problems with alcohol and drug use is characterized by:

- a strong desire to take alcohol or drugs
- difficulty in controlling use
- associated problems due to drug and alcohol use.

The key feature is a desire to take psychoactive drugs, alcohol, or tobacco. The desire is often strong and sometimes overpowering. For example:

> Amanda has used cannabis at the weekend for three years. Last month she began using it daily. Amanda is 20 years old. She wishes she could resist using cannabis daily but the desire to use the drug feels overpowering. The cannabis use is starting to interfere with her life; she is spending a lot of money on cannabis, is arriving late for her job, and is having trouble remembering things.

Why do some people develop problems with alcohol and drugs while others do not? How do we respond? These questions are complex and intriguing, so simple answers should not be expected. Addiction is determined by multiple interacting factors. It is the unravelling of these factors that provides a challenge to addiction research.

What is a drug?

A drug is a chemical agent, other than food, that affects biological function in humans or other animals. A psychotropic drug is one that acts in the brain to alter mood, thought processes, or behaviour. Table 1.1 presents a list of psychotropic drugs and their "street" names.

The current *Diagnostic and Statistical Manual of the American Psychiatric Association* (DSM-IV) has defined a number of classes of drugs that may be part of a substance use disorder (American Psychiatric Association, 1994). These are, in alphabetical order: alcohol, caffeine, cannabis, hallucinogens, heroin and other opiates,

TABLE 1.1

A brief list of "street" drug names (USA, UK, and Australia)

Drug type	Common names
Cannabinoids	Acapulco gold, afghani, a stick, bhang, boo, bomb, brick, buddha sticks, dope, columbian, ganja, gold, grass, hash, hashish, hay, hemp, J, jane, jive, joint, key, marijuana, mexican, MJ, oil, pot, reefer, rope, stick, thai sticks, THC, weed
Cocaine	Blow, C, charlie, coke, crack, dust, dynamite, flake, gold dust, heaven dust, lady, nose, nose candy, rock, snow, speedball, toot, white
Amphetamines	Bennies, blue angels, chris, crystal, ecstacy, ice, meth, pinks, speed, speedball (heroin and cocaine), uppers, ups, whites
Hallucinogens and psychedelics	Acid, blue dots, blue meanies, goldtops, ketamine, LSD, magic mushrooms, mesc, microdot, psilocybin, special K, tabs, trips, white lightening
Inhalants and solvents	Glue, petrol, nitrous oxide, laughing gas, amyl nitrate, rush, ethyl
Sedatives and tranquillizers	Amies, blue birds, blue devils, blue heaven, blues, bullets, candy, dolls, barbiturates, barbs, downers, downs, librium, mogadon, normison, quads, rohypnol, serepax, sleepers, sleeping pills, tranqs, yellows, valium, xanax
Opioids: Analgesics and others	Brown, black (opium), cat, codeine, doloxene, H, homebake, heroin, horse, junk, methadone, morphine, percodan, pethidine, poppy, scat, skag, smack, tar
Phencyclidine (PCP)	Angel, cheap cocaine, green, K, mist, purple, supercoke, supergrass, whack

inhalants, nicotine, phencyclidine (PCP), sedatives and stimulants (cocaine and amphetamines).

This book focuses on the following five major classes of drugs: alcohol, nicotine, cannabis, opioids, and stimulants. Problems with the use of these drugs have the greatest social and economic impact on society, and the use of these drugs also contributes to many life-threatening disorders. The term "drug" is used hereafter to encompass all five substances. Non-drug addictions, such as problem gambling, eating, and sexual behaviour, are not addressed in this book.

Effects of drugs

Each class of drugs has different short-term or immediate effects and longer-term effects. These effects can be different from person to person, and are most often related to a person's size and the potency of the drug being consumed. The short-term and long-term effects are outlined below for each of the major classes of drugs.

- *Alcohol*: The short-term effects of alcohol are well known and include loss of inhibitions, lack of coordination and slower reaction time, blurred vision and slurred speech, aggression. Excessive use of alcohol can result in coma and death.
- *Nicotine*: The short-term effects of nicotine include increased pulse rate, temporary rise in blood pressure, acid in the stomach, decreased blood flow to body extremities (such as fingers and toes), nausea, and watery eyes. The long-term use of nicotine can lead to a reduction in a person's sense of smell and taste, premature and more abundant face wrinkles, and increased risk of colds, chronic bronchitis, emphysema, heart disease, and certain types of cancer.
- *Cannabis*: The short-term effects of cannabis include euphoria, increased talking and laughing, sleepiness, loss of coordination and concentration, loss of inhibitions and a feeling of well-being, bloodshot eyes, anxiety and paranoia, increased appetite and dryness of the mouth and throat. The long-term use of cannabis can lead to an increased risk of respiratory diseases associated with smoking, decreased learning and memory abilities, decreased motivation in areas such as study, work or concentration and accidental injury.
- *Heroin*: The short-term effects of heroin include euphoria, relief of pain, and a feeling of well-being. Heroin use can also result in nausea and vomiting, constipation, and sleepiness. The long-term effects include lowered sex drive, impotence in men and infertility in women, risk of hepatitis and AIDS through injection, death by overdose. The effects of heroin use are described in the following example:

> After you fix it you feel the rush, like an orgasm if it's good dope. Then you float for about four hours; nothing positive, just a normal feeling, nowhere. It's like being half asleep, like watching a movie; nothing gets through to you, you're safe and warm. The big

thing is you don't hurt. You can walk around with rotting teeth and a busted appendix and not feel it. You don't need sex, you don't need food, you don't need people, you don't care. It's like death without permanence, life without pain.

(Case study of Ed from Smith and Gay, 197, p. 145)

- *Cocaine*: The short-term effects of a stimulant such as cocaine include increased blood pressure, heart rate, breathing rate and body temperature, increased alertness and energy, an extreme feeling of well-being, sexual arousal, dilated pupils, and loss of appetite. The long-term effects of cocaine include sleeping disorders, sexual problems, heart attacks, strokes and respiratory failure, as well as nosebleeds, sinusitus and tearing of the nasal wall resulting from snorting, and hepatitis or human immuno-deficiency virus (HIV) through shared needles.
- *Amphetamines*: The short-term effects of amphetamines include euphoria and a feeling of well-being, increased blood pressure and pulse rate, sweating, jaw-clenching and teeth-grinding, nausea and anxiety. The long-term effects of amphetamines include sleeping problems including insomnia, appetite suppression, high blood pressure, and rapid and irregular heart beat (National Drug and Alcohol Research Centre, 1999).
- *Benzodiazepines*: The short-term effects of benzodiazepines include drowsiness and lethargy, dizziness and blurred or double vision, mental confusion and mood swings, memory loss and slurred speech. The long-term effects include lethargy and lack of motivation, loss of sexual interest and function, increased appetite and weight gain, menstrual problems and skin rashes (National Drug and Alcohol Research Centre, 1999).

People use drugs for many reasons, but report that the main reason is to make them "feel better". Not everyone who uses drugs, including alcohol, will be adversely affected, so why do some people have problems while others do not? This is the focus of the next section.

What causes problems with alcohol and other drugs?

There is a perennial debate among researchers about what causes addiction problems with alcohol or other drugs: Is it a chronic disease or a learnt behaviour (learnt from your family or peers). Historically, addiction has been viewed as a chronic disease. An individual was considered to have the disease if he or she lacked the willpower to stop the excessive use of alcohol and other drugs. The only cure was considered to be a complete abstinence from alcohol or other drug use.

In contrast, modern theories see addiction as the consequence of chronic heavy alcohol or drug use. This heavy use is argued to arise from an interaction between an individual's genes and his or her environment. Once the person develops heavy drug use, addiction is the next stage.

The first step in unravelling addiction is to define clearly what is meant by the term "addiction". What does it mean to say that a person has a problem with alcohol or drugs? In 1970, Griffith Edwards and colleagues were the first to provide a clinical description of alcohol dependence (Edwards, Arif, & Hodgson, 1981; Edwards & Gross, 1976; Edwards, Gross, Keller, Moser, & Room, 1977). Edwards and Gross suggested that "alcoholics" exhibited a characteristic cluster of symptoms that could be used to diagnose addiction to alcohol. They developed this concept after carefully observing the patients they had seen in their treatment clinics. The symptoms they observed included a strong desire to drink, requiring more drink to get the same effect, and withdrawal symptoms when the intake of alcohol stopped.

A related concept of dependence was then included in the *Diagnostic and Statistical Manual of the American Psychiatric Association*. According to the DSM definition, dependence is a compulsion to use a drug that is not medically necessary, accompanied by impairment in health or social functioning (American Psychiatric Association, 1994; World Health Organization, 1993). The term "drug dependence" as used in these classifications is equivalent to the more popular term "addiction".

Edwards et al. (1977) suggested that alcohol dependence could be defined by a repeating cluster of signs and symptoms that occurred in heavy drinkers and could be conceptually distinguished from alcohol-related problems. Seven factors were regarded as major symptoms of alcohol dependence.

1. Narrowing of the behavioural repertoire: For example, an individual who is dependent may only drink one or two types of alcoholic drink in the same way on weekdays and weekends.
2. Salience of drinking or drug use: With increasing dependence the individual gives greater priority to substance use.

3. Subjective awareness of a compulsion: The individual experiences loss of control over the substance use, and has an inability to stop using the substance.
4. Increased tolerance: The individual uses more of the substance to get the same effects or the same amount of the substance has less effect.
5. Repeated withdrawal symptoms: These include fatigue or exhaustion, sweating, diarrhoea, anxious, depressed, irritable, restless, trouble sleeping, tremors, stomach ache, headache, weakness, nausea or vomiting, fits, muscle aches or cramps, runny eyes or nose, yawning, intense craving, seeing things that are not really there, heart beating fast, change in appetite, fever.
6. Relief or avoidance of withdrawal symptoms by further drinking: The individual uses substances in order to stop withdrawal symptoms (e.g., morning drinking).
7. Reinstatement of dependent drinking after abstinence: A rapid return to dependent drinking after a period of abstinence.

There has been much research on the description and classification of problems with alcohol and they have been shown to be reasonably close to clinical reality (Babor, Orrock, Liebowitz, Salomon, & Brown, 1990). Furthermore, and importantly, it has been shown to be applicable to other drugs (Cottler, Phelps, & Crompton, 1995). These classification systems are outlined in the following section and form the basis of internationally agreed criteria for diagnosing problems associated with alcohol and other drugs.

Diagnosing problems

One of the most widely used classificatory system for psychological disorders is the DSM-IV (*Diagnostic and Statistical Manual of Mental Disorders*, 4th edition). The DSM-IV provides criteria for diagnosing drug abuse and drug dependence and these are outlined below.

Diagnosing abuse

Criteria for substance abuse

A. A maladaptive pattern of substance use leading to clinically significant impairment or distress, as manifested by one (or more) of the following, occurring within a 12-month period:

(1) recurrent substance use resulting in a failure to fulfil major role obligations at work, school, or home (e.g., repeated absences or poor work performance related to substance use; substance-related absences, suspensions, or expulsions from school; neglect of children or household)

(2) recurrent substance use in situations in which it is physically hazardous (e.g., driving an automobile or operating a machine when impaired by substance use)

(3) recurrent substance-related legal problems (e.g., arrests for substance-related disorderly conduct)

(4) continued substance use despite having persistent or recurrent social or interpersonal problems caused or exacerbated by the effects of substance (e.g., arguments with spouse about consequences of intoxication, physical fights).

B. The symptoms have never met the criteria for substance dependence for this class of substance.

(American Psychiatric Association, 1994, pp. 182–183)

Diagnosing dependence

For drug dependence under the DSM-IV system, at least three of seven key symptoms must be met. The key symptoms for diagnosis of drug dependence are outlined below. In addition to outlining the criteria that relate to substance dependence generally, DSM-IV also describes the specific aspects of dependence for 11 classes of substances.

Criteria for substance dependence

A maladaptive pattern of substance abuse, leading to clinically significant impairment or distress, as manifested by three or more of the following, occurring at any time in the same 12-month period:

(1) tolerance, as defined by either of the following:
   (a) a need for markedly increased amounts of the substance to achieve intoxication or desired effect

    (b)   markedly diminished effect with continued use of the same amount of the substance
(2) withdrawal, as manifested by either of the following:
    (a)   the characteristic withdrawal syndrome for the substance
    (b)   the same (or a closely related) substance is taken to relieve or avoid withdrawal symptoms
(3) the substance is often taken in larger amounts or over a longer period than was intended
(4) there is a persistent desire or unsuccessful efforts to cut down or to control substance use
(5) a great deal of time is spent in activities necessary to obtain the substance, use the substance (e.g., chain smoking), or recover from its effects
(6) important social, occupational, or recreational activities are given up or reduced because of substance abuse
(7) the substance use is continued despite knowledge of having a persistent or recurrent physical or psychological problem that is likely to have been caused or exacerbated by the substance.

(American Psychiatric Association, 1994, p. 176)

The experience of dependence and abuse on a drug can be very different for different individuals and across different drug classes and is illustrated in the following cases:

Ecstasy abuse: Dana is a university student who takes ecstasy most weekends when she goes out clubbing with friends. Despite trying to limit the amount she spends on drugs, at times she gets carried away and spends money meant for food and bills on pills for a night out. When this happens Dana ends up having to borrow money for food until she next gets paid. Dana often skips classes on Mondays because she has not yet recovered from the weekend.

Alcohol dependence: Jeff is a 26-year-old male who presented to his general practitioner because he had been missing work due to hangovers from his alcohol use. He is married with two children. His wife encouraged him to ask his general practitioner about his drinking.

Jeff had begun drinking at the age of 15 years and started regular consumption at 18 years. By the time he was 20 years old, he was drinking four to six beers regularly through the week and on Friday and Saturday nights. In the last year he had begun binge drinking, drinking up to 15 or more standard drinks. He was also drinking the next day in order to recover.

His recent alcohol use was two standard drinks of beer before work, eight at lunch and another five standard drinks of beer after work. His GP did a medical examination and had some liver enzyme levels analysed. While Jeff's liver was not enlarged, there were elevated levels of a number of liver enzymes, confirming Jeff's heavy drinking.

Drug use can be sporadic, as seen in the case of Dana above, or more chronic and long term, as with Jeff's alcohol use. Both are experiencing problems and it is affecting not only themselves but also their friends, work, and family. Many people will use alcohol and drugs, some will experience problems, and others will not. A person may be having a problem with drugs if he or she has:

- a strong desire to take alcohol or drugs
- difficulty controlling use
- associated problems due to drug and alcohol use.

The amount of use that is acceptable to different cultural groups and cultures varies, as do the associated problems that are acceptable. This is particularly the case for alcohol. While there are no norms for safe levels of use for illicit substances, many countries have developed guidelines for the safe consumption of alcohol. The cultural and societal aspects of alcohol use are considered in the next section.

The following quick quiz is useful in assessing problems with cannabis use:

"Are you addicted to cannabis?"

Answer the following questions as honestly as you can:

1. Has smoking pot stopped being fun?
2. Do you ever get high alone?
3. Is it hard for you to imagine life without dope?

4. Do you find that your friends are deterred by your marijuana use?
5. Do you smoke marijuana to avoid dealing with your problems?
6. Do you smoke pot to change or enhance your feelings?
7. Does your marijuana use let you live in a privately defined world?
8. Have you ever failed to keep promises you made about cutting down or controlling your dope smoking?
9. Do you have difficulty remembering what you said or did?
10. When your stash is nearly empty, do you feel anxious or worried about how to get more?
11. Do you plan your life around your marijuana use?
12. Have friends or relatives ever complained that your pot smoking is damaging your relationship with them?

If you answered "Yes" to any of the above questions then your marijuana use may be problematic.

Cultural factors and attitudes to drugs

The drinking and drug-taking behaviour of individuals and societies always occurs in the context of norms, attitudes, and values. Thus, there are variations between cultural groups with regard to the types of substances and the level of substance use that is considered to be acceptable (Heath, 2000). Attitudes to alcohol provide a good example of the variation that occurs across cultures. In some societies – for example, among certain religious groups – it is generally agreed that no one should drink, and those individuals who do are treated as deviant or abnormal. While in other societies – for example, in France – it is expected that everyone will drink, and those individuals who do not are considered unusual and in some cases suspect (Heath, 2000).

Cultural variation regarding what is considered to be an acceptable level of alcohol intake is reflected in the guidelines for moderate drinking that are published by governments in countries around the world. To cite the extremes, the Canadian Committee on Health and

Welfare recommend daily consumption of 13.5 grams of ethanol equivalents for both men and women, while in the Basque Country of Spain, the Department of Health and Social security recommend daily consumption of 70 grams of ethanol equivalents for men and 28 grams for women.

Who becomes addicted? 2

Epidemiology

For many years addiction was considered to be a relatively rare disorder with a poor outcome: few individuals were thought to become abstinent, and many died from the medical complications of their drug use. As these views were mostly formed from studies of people who seek treatment they were biased since few people seek treatment for addiction, and those that do are usually severely addicted. More recently, a number of large epidemiological studies of addiction in the general population have challenged these pessimistic views and the results of some of these studies are reported below.

The US Epidemiologic Catchment Area study

The Epidemiologic Catchment Area (ECA) study is the first large epidemiological study to examine problems with alcohol and other drugs in the general community. It involved personal interviews with 20,000 Americans in Baltimore, Maryland; Los Angeles, California; New Haven, Connecticut; Durham, North Carolina; and St Louis, Missouri (Regier et al., 1990, 1993; Robins & Regier, 1991). A standardized interview for detecting the presence or absence of mental disorders was used in 40 major psychiatric diagnoses, including alcohol and drug dependence.

In this study a diagnosis of *alcohol abuse* required excessive or uncontrolled alcohol use and impairment in social or occupational functioning due to alcohol use. *Alcohol dependence* required evidence of either excessive or uncontrolled drinking, or social and occupational impairment (or both), and evidence of either tolerance or withdrawal (or both), consistent with the DSM-IV criteria described previously.

Alcohol use disorders (alcohol abuse and/or dependence) were the second most common mental disorder (Helzer, Burnam, & McEvoy, 1991). One in seven people had had an alcohol use disorder at some time in their lives. As expected, men were more likely to have an alcohol use disorder than women: 24% of men and 5% of women had an alcohol use disorder at some time in their lives. Alcohol use disorders were more common in younger people (Helzer et al., 1991).

The ECA study showed that the more you drank (exposure to heavy drinking) the greater your risk of developing an alcohol use disorder. The lifetime experience of a disorder increased from 15% among all drinkers to 49% of those with a history of drinking more than seven drinks in a session at least once a week. Differences in exposure to heavy drinking probably explain the differences in lifetime rates between men and women and younger and older persons. Men were much more likely to experience heavy drinking and, with changes in social values, younger people were also more likely than older people to be exposed to heavy drinking.

Other mental disorders, such as depression and anxiety, were also common in people with alcohol use disorders. Nearly half the people with alcohol use disorders (47%) also had a second psychiatric diagnosis. The most common such diagnoses were: drug abuse and dependence, antisocial personality disorder, mania, schizophrenia, panic disorders, and obsessive–compulsive disorders (Helzer et al., 1991).

Alcohol dependence in the ECA was "a disorder of youthful onset", with 80% of those who have ever experienced a symptom having done so before the age of 30. It was also a disorder with a high rate of remission: half of those who had ever experienced a symptom had not experienced one for at least a year. The average length of symptoms was less than five years, indicating that many who drink heavily and experience symptoms of dependence can stop drinking for periods of a year or more. Importantly, most individuals who stopped or moderated their drinking did so without professional assistance. Only 12% had ever told a doctor about their drinking problem.

This large epidemiological study showed that alcohol use disorders in the community have a more benign outcome than the pessimistic picture we obtain from clinical populations, which contain a preponderance of individuals who have failed to stop drinking by their own efforts.

The ECA study (Regier et al., 1990, 1993; Robins & Regier, 1991) also estimated the prevalence of drug abuse and dependence in the community. Illicit drug use was defined as "any nonprescription psychoactive agents other than tobacco, alcohol and caffeine, or inappropriate use of prescription drugs". Individuals had to have used an illicit drug on more than five occasions before they were asked about any symptoms of drug abuse dependence.

A diagnosis of *drug abuse* required a pattern of pathological use and impaired functioning (defined in the same way as alcohol abuse) while a diagnosis of *drug dependence* required only tolerance or withdrawal (except in the case of cannabis, where a diagnosis of dependence required pathological use, or impaired social functioning, and either tolerance or withdrawal). The problem had to have been present for at least one month.

One in three in the ECA sample (36%) had used one or more illicit drugs. Cannabis was the most commonly used illicit drug (having been used by almost one in three Americans). Drug abuse and dependence (hereafter drug use disorders) were diagnosed in 6% of the population, with cannabis affecting 4% of the population, followed by stimulants (2%), sedatives (1%), and opioid drugs (0.7%). Men had higher rates of drug use disorders than women, and the highest rate was in the 18–29-year age group.

As was true of alcohol use disorders, exposure to illicit drug use was the most likely reason for the differences in rates between men and women and younger and older persons. The low rates of drug use disorders among adults over the age of 40 reflects the recency of widespread illicit drug use in US society.

There was also a high rate of other mental problems among those with drug use disorders. Over two-thirds (76% of men and 65% of women) had a second psychiatric diagnosis. The most common diagnoses were alcohol use disorders (60% of men and 30% of women) and antisocial personality disorder (22% of men and 10% of women).

Little information was provided on the remission of drug use disorders because of their relative youth and hence the shorter duration of their disorders. As with alcohol use disorders, only a minority of those who had a diagnosis of drug use disorders had mentioned their drug problem to a health professional.

The US National Comorbidity Survey

The most recent US study of alcohol and drug problems is the National Comorbidity Survey (NCS). This survey examined the extent of comorbidity between substance use and non-substance use disorders in the USA between 1990 and 1992. The NCS aimed to improve on the earlier ECA in a number of respects. First, it provided prevalence estimates of major disorders as defined in the newly revised DSM-III-R (American Psychiatric Association, 1987) classification. Second, more detail was obtained on risk factors for specific disorders. Third, the study aimed to achieve a nationally representative sample of the US population rather than, as in the ECA study, representative samples from catchment areas that were not representative of the US population. Fourth, special efforts were made to ensure that the rate of non-response was as low as possible, and additional efforts were made to estimate the effect of non-response on estimates of the population prevalence of mental disorders. The achieved sample was 8,098, which represented an 83% response rate, compared to 76% for the ECA study. Adjustment was made for non-response because studies of those who initially refused to be interviewed suggested that rates of mental disorder were higher among non-responders.

The NCS produced a higher lifetime prevalence of any mental disorder than the ECA, and a higher prevalence of depressive disorders. It would appear that the major reasons for this result were: (a) the NCS sample was younger, and hence contained more persons with mental disorders that generally commence in early adult life; (b) the NCS estimates were corrected for non-response, which increased the overall rates; and (c) a number of changes were made to the way in which the measurement instrument enquired about symptoms of phobias and depressive disorders that were likely to increase the rate of reporting. There was much better agreement between the NCS and ECA in the prevalence of mental disorders in the past year and there was a consistent gender difference in pattern of disorders.

The NCS differed from the ECA in assessing dependence symptoms in any person who had used any of the listed drug types on at least one occasion (as against five or more times in the ECA). It also widened its coverage of types of drug dependence to include tobacco for half of the sample. Of all those who had ever used a drug, this permitted an estimate of the proportion that had met criteria for dependence on it during their lifetimes.

The prevalence estimates showed the following proportions of the population that had met lifetime criteria for dependence on tobacco (24%), alcohol (14%), any controlled substance (7.5%), cannabis (4%), cocaine (3%), psychostimulants (2%), anxiolytics (1%), and heroin (0.4%). These proportions are affected by the prevalence of use of these substances, so it is more informative to examine the proportions of those who had ever used a drug who met the criteria for dependence on it. These were: 32% for tobacco, 23% for opiates, 17% for cocaine, 15% for alcohol, 11% for psychostimulants, 9% for anxiolytics, and 9% for cannabis.

Rates of comorbidity were high among those with a diagnosis of alcohol dependence: 78% of men and 86% of women with this diagnosis had another mental disorder. The highest comorbidity were with other forms of drug dependence, affective disorders (mostly major depression and dysthymia), and anxiety disorders.

The UK Mental Health Survey

A UK household survey of mental disorders has recently been conducted (Meltzer, Gill, Petticrew, & Hinds, 1995). However, it examined the prevalence of symptoms within the previous month and did not diagnose disorders in terms of the ICD-10 or DSM-IV, so its results are difficult to compare directly with the ECA or NCS in the USA. Insofar as can be judged, the overall prevalence of symptoms, their rank ordering, and the pattern of symptoms related to age and gender are similar to those of the ECA and NCS.

The Australian National Survey of Mental Health and Well-Being

The National Survey of Mental Health and Well-Being (NSMHWB; Australian Bureau of Statistics, 1998; Hall, Teesson, Lynskey, & Degenhardt, 1998b, 1999c; Teesson, Hall, Lynskey, & Degenhardt, 2000a) was the first national survey of the prevalence of common mental disorders in the Australian adult general population. The survey interviewed a representative sample of 10,641 adults (aged 18 years or older) from throughout Australia and assessed symptoms of the affective, anxiety, and substance use disorders. Disorders were defined in terms of ICD-10 and DSM-IV diagnostic criteria. Substance use disorders included harmful use and dependence on alcohol, and the harmful use and dependence on four classes of drug: cannabis, stimulants, sedatives, and opioids.

In the past 12 months, 6.5% of Australians 18 years and over had an ICD-10 alcohol use disorder, and 2.2% had some other drug use

Figure 2.1. Prevalence (%) of alcohol and drug use disorders by age and gender.

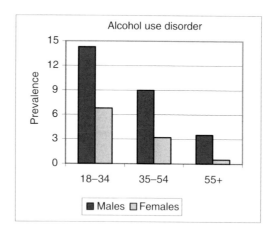

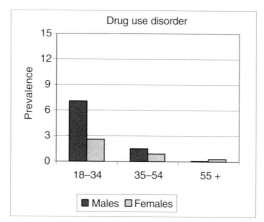

disorder. More males than females had alcohol and other drug use disorders and, as in the ECA and NCS, the prevalence of substance use disorders decreased with increasing age. This consistent world-wide trend is shown in Figure 2.1.

Alcohol was the most widely used of any drug but more users of other drugs had a use disorder in the past year. Specifically, only 8.9% of those who used alcohol in the previous 12 months had an alcohol use disorder while 22.7% of those who used other drugs had a different drug use disorder.

One in four of the adult Australian population (25%) reported current regular tobacco use (at least once a day). Rates of tobacco use were higher among males (27.1%) than females (23.1%), and there was a steady decrease in regular tobacco use with age: 33.4% of respondents aged 18–34 years were regular smokers compared to 13.8% of those 55 years or older.

Summary

The epidemiological surveys tell us much about who becomes addicted. Across different countries the surveys consistently show that men are much more likely than women to become addicted and this is probably because they are exposed to heavier alcohol use and more drug-taking. The studies also show that, contrary to popular belief, alcohol dependence is experienced by the young at greater rates than older persons and is a disorder of youthful onset (younger than 30 years). However, the disorder has high remission rates. Of the illicit drugs used across the epidemiological studies, cannabis is the most common.

The health consequences of alcohol and other drug dependence 3

Persons who are dependent on alcohol and other drugs are at high risk of experiencing adverse consequences of their drug use, including health problems, violence, and accidents. However, the relationship between dependence and harm to health is not perfect. Not all drug-dependent persons develop serious adverse health consequences. For example, healthy young adults may drink heavily enough to meet criteria for alcohol dependence but cease their hazardous use of alcohol before serious health complications develop. Nor are all adverse health effects of alcohol and other drugs confined to people who are alcohol or drug dependent. Accidental injuries, drownings, falls, and violence may occur among intoxicated young adults who are not alcohol dependent. Nonetheless, an overview of the major health consequences of alcohol and other drug dependence can be obtained by reviewing the major adverse health consequences that have been linked to the use of these drugs.

As an example, English et al. (1995) have estimated the harm caused to health by alcohol, tobacco, and illicit drug use in Australia in 1992. They assessed this in terms of the number of premature deaths attributed to each drug, the number of life years lost as a result of these deaths, and the number of hospital bed days spent treating conditions caused by alcohol, tobacco, and illicit drugs.

They assumed that the use of these drugs was a contributory cause of injury, illness, and death; that is, drug use was one component of a large set of conditions that bring about the specific adverse health effect. Drug use was assumed to be probabilistically related to injury,

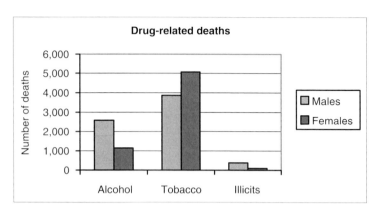

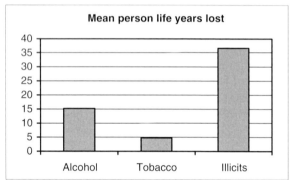

illness, and death. The exception was the minority of conditions that are aetiologically defined in terms of drug use, such as alcoholic liver cirrhosis, drug-induced psychosis, and opiate dependence. In these cases, the proportion of cases attributed to drug use is 100%.

English et al. (1995) estimated from epidemiological studies the proportion of each specific condition that was attributable to drug use. These estimates were then multiplied by the number of deaths, hospital episodes, and bed days for each specific condition in Australia in 1992, and these products were summed to produce an overall estimate of the number of deaths, life years lost, and hospital bed days that were attributed to each form of drug use.

They found that tobacco produced the greatest premature mortality, life years lost, and hospital bed days, followed by alcohol and illicit drugs (see Figures 3.1 and 3.2). Tobacco caused many more deaths than alcohol or illicit drugs. There was less of a gap between tobacco and alcohol and illicit drugs in terms of life years lost because alcohol and illicit drugs adversely affect health at an earlier age than

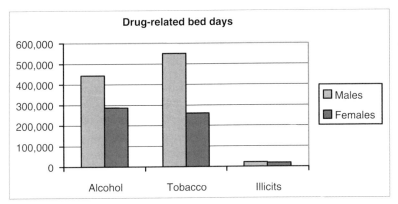

Figure 3.2. Drug-related bed days in Australia 1992.

tobacco. The difference between alcohol and tobacco narrowed further in terms of hospital bed days because chronic alcohol-related conditions begin to affect adults in middle life.

Alcohol-related mortality and morbidity

Mortality, life years lost, and hospital morbidity attributed to alcohol use were all much higher for males than for females in all age groups, reflecting higher rates of hazardous and harmful alcohol use among males. There were interesting differences between men and women in the contribution of the acute effects of alcohol intoxication and the effects of sustained heavy alcohol use. In males the largest contributions were made by: deaths attributable to injury, particularly motor vehicle accidents, falls, and drowning (29% of male deaths); gastrointestinal diseases, particularly liver cirrhosis (24%); cardiovascular disease, particularly stroke (19%); and suicide and assaults (12%). In women, the largest contributions were made by stroke (38%), injury (28%), and gastrointestinal disease (15%).

In terms of life years lost, the picture for males was dominated by injury, violence, and cirrhosis. This reflected the young average age of males dying from alcohol-related accidents, suicide, and assault. For women, differences in the contribution of these specific causes was less marked, with injury and violence predominating.

In terms of hospital bed days, alcohol made a major contribution of accidental injury among younger age groups, while treatment for alcohol dependence and alcoholic psychoses made a major contribution in older age groups.

In the foetus, heavy chronic alcohol use can cause Foetal Alcohol Syndrome (FAS). The baby has distinctive facial features and may be mentally and developmentally retarded. However, most women can drink in moderation during pregnancy and not have a child with FAS.

Tobacco-related mortality and morbidity

Tobacco was responsible for more deaths, life years lost, and hospital bed days in males than in females at all ages. This reflects the higher prevalence of cigarette-smoking among males until recently. Deaths attributable to cigarette-smoking in men and women began much later than those attributable to alcohol, first becoming apparent in the 1950s, and increasing through the 1960s and 1970s. Nonetheless, the life years lost because of tobacco-smoking were still substantial. Even though the average age at death from tobacco-related causes was higher, the number of persons affected by tobacco-related diseases was large so that, in aggregate, tobacco accounted for a large number of life years lost.

The impact of tobacco smoking on hospital bed days occurred at an earlier age than deaths. Smokers' health begins to deteriorate as a result of respiratory and heart disease some decades before these diseases kill many of them. In men the largest contributions to tobacco-related death were made by: cardiovascular disease, particularly ischaemic heart disease (38%); cancers, particularly lung cancer (37%); and respiratory diseases, particularly chronic obstructive lung disease (24%). Among women, the pattern of causes was very similar.

Among men and women, cardiovascular disease and cancer make a larger contribution to life years lost than respiratory disease that strikes later in life and produces more chronic illness.

Cardiovascular disease dominated tobacco-related morbidity in males and females, followed by respiratory disease, and then cancers. Effects of maternal smoking during pregnancy on the health of mothers and infants had an impact on hospital morbidity that was not reflected in mortality or life years lost.

Illicit drug-related mortality and morbidity

We do not know as much about causal relationships between illicit drug use and health as we do about tobacco and alcohol. Direct, acute drug effects such as drug overdose and drug-induced psychosis are known but their contribution is probably underestimated because of underdiagnosis. The contribution of illicit drugs to chronic disease and injury is probably also underestimated because of the paucity of data on the long-term effects of their use (Hall, Solowij, & Lemon, 1994).

Illicit drug use accounts for a smaller number of deaths than alcohol and tobacco but produces a larger number of life years lost per death because many deaths among illicit drug users occur in their twenties and thirties. Hospitalization attributable to illicit drug use is also concentrated in the same young age groups, with the addition of the effects of maternal drug use on babies and infants.

The major cause of death attributable to illicit drug use in Australia in 1992 was opiate "overdose", which accounted for 92% of male and 89% of female illicit drug deaths. Injecting drug use is also a major vector for the transmission of infectious diseases, such as human immunodeficiency virus (HIV) and hepatitis B and C (inflammation of the liver). HIV is the causative agent of acquired immune deficiency syndrome (AIDS). HIV causes the death of lymphatic and neural cells and an infected person is no longer able to fight infections. A person has AIDS when he or she acquires an infection or disease (e.g., pneumonia) to which the body has no resistance because of the HIV. These causes of death and hospitalization were low in Australia, but much higher in the USA and parts of Europe. Other forms of illicit drug use accounted for a minority of all deaths attributable to illicit drug use in Australia. In countries with high rates of cocaine use, more deaths are attributed to cocaine toxicity.

Illicit opiate use accounted for most hospital bed days attributed to illicit drugs in Australia. Drug-induced psychosis, which is probably due to stimulant use, makes a larger contribution to hospital morbidity and is followed by stimulant-related admissions, which is consistent with the high rates of psychological and other morbidity reported among illicit amphetamine users. Cannabis use also makes a contribution to hospital morbidity but it makes no known contribution to mortality or life years lost.

Adverse health and psychological effects of cannabis use

The major acute psychological and health effects of cannabis intoxication are: anxiety, dysphoria, and panic in naive users (Hall &

Solowij, 1998; Hall et al., 1994); cognitive and psychomotor impairment while intoxicated (Hall et al., 1994), and probably an increased risk of accidental injury if an intoxicated person drives a motor vehicle or operates machinery (Hall et al., 1994); an increased risk at very high doses of experiencing psychotic symptoms, and perhaps at lower doses among those with a personal or family history of psychosis (Hall, 1998); and an increased risk of low-birth-weight babies if cannabis is smoked during pregnancy (Hall et al., 1994).

The major health and psychological effects of chronic cannabis use over many years are less certain because of the comparative absence of evidence from prospective or case-control studies (Hall & Solowij, 1998). The most probable adverse health effects appear to be: respiratory diseases associated with smoking, such as chronic bronchitis; development of a cannabis dependence syndrome, characterized by a loss of control over cannabis use (Hall et al., 1994); subtle forms of cognitive impairment that persist while the user remains chronically intoxicated, and may not reverse after abstinence (Hall et al., 1994); and exacerbation of psychotic symptoms in individuals with schizophrenia (Hall, 1998).

There are also a number of possible adverse effects of chronic, heavy cannabis use that remain to be confirmed by better controlled studies. These are: an increased risk of cancers of the oral cavity, pharynx, and oesophagus (Hall et al., 1994); leukaemia among the offspring of women who used cannabis during pregnancy (Hall et al., 1994); and reduced educational attainment in adolescents (Lynskey & Hall, 2000).

There are a number of groups at higher risk for problems associated with cannabis use. Adolescents with a history of poor school performance may have their educational achievement further limited by the cognitive impairments produced by chronic cannabis intoxication (Lynskey & Hall, 2000). Adolescents who initiate cannabis use in their early teens are at higher risk of progressing to other illicit drug use, and to becoming dependent on cannabis (Hall et al., 1994).

Pregnant women who smoke cannabis are probably at increased risk of giving birth to low-birth-weight babies, and perhaps of shortening their period of gestation (Hall et al., 1994). Women of child-bearing age who smoke cannabis while trying to conceive or while pregnant possibly increase the risk of their children being born with birth defects (Hall et al., 1994).

Persons with a number of pre-existing diseases who smoke cannabis are probably at an increased risk of exacerbating symptoms of their diseases. These include: individuals with cardiovascular diseases; individuals with respiratory diseases; individuals with schizophrenia; and individuals who are or have been dependent on alcohol and other drugs (Hall et al., 1994).

Adverse health and psychological effects of amphetamine use

Amphetamine users who inject the drug are at risk of contracting blood-borne infections through sharing needles and equipment, and are as likely as opioid users to share injection equipment (Hall & Hando, 1993; Loxley, Carruthers, & Bevan, 1995). The social nature of amphetamine use also means that users may be more frequently placed in high-risk situations. The risk of infection among amphetamine users is higher than in past epidemics of amphetamine use in Australia, when the drug was typically used by non-parenteral routes (Hall & Hando, 1993). In addition, the youth of amphetamine users places them at risk of sexual transmission of diseases such as HIV and hepatitis B (although not hepatitis C). Primary amphetamine injectors are a sexually active group, and a small proportion engages in paid sex to support drug use (Hall & Hando, 1993).

High-dose amphetamine use, especially by injection, can result in a schizophreniform paranoid psychosis, associated with loosening of associations, delusions, and hallucinations (Gawin & Kleber, 1986) and high proportions of regular amphetamine users report anxiety, panic attacks, paranoia, and depression (Hall, 1996). All of these symptoms have been shown to be associated with injecting the drugs, greater frequency of use, and dependence on amphetamines (Hall, 1996).

In sufficiently high doses amphetamines can be lethal (Derlet, Rice, Horowitz, & Lord, 1989); however, the risk of fatal overdose is low compared to the risks of opioid overdose. Typically, amphetamine-related deaths are caused by abnormalities in the cardiovascular system – e.g., cardiac failure and cerebral vascular accidents (Mattick & Darke, 1995) – and deficits in performance on neuropsychological tests have been demonstrated among Australian amphetamine users, suggesting that amphetamines are also neurotoxic (McKetin & Mattick, 1997, 1998).

Adverse health and psychological effects of cocaine use

In the USA, cocaine injecting, either alone or in combination with heroin ("speedballs"), is strongly associated with more frequent injections, more frequent needle-sharing, increased sexual risk-taking, more frequent use of shooting galleries, and a higher rate of HIV infection (Chaisson, Osmond, Brodie, Sande, & Moss, 1989). The association between cocaine use and HIV risk-taking has also been reported in Europe (Torrens, San, Peri, & Olle, 1991) and Australia (Darke, Baker, Dixon, Wodak, & Heather, 1992).

In the USA regular cocaine use has been strongly associated with high rates of anxiety and affective disorders (cf. Platt, 1997). As is the case with amphetamines, the repeated administration of cocaine is also associated with the development of a schizophreniform psychosis (Majewska, 1996; Manschreck, 1993; Platt, 1997).

While not as toxic as opioids, cocaine can be fatal in large doses (Platt, 1997). As it is cardiotoxic, it places a strain on the cardio-vascular system and overdose can cause cardiac arrest and cerebral vascular accidents (Majewska, 1996; Platt, 1997). As is the case with amphetamines, cocaine use also appears to be neurotoxic (Majewska, 1996; Platt, 1997).

Adverse health and psychological effects of heroin use

The adverse health consequences of heroin use include: heroin dependence; contracting blood-borne infectious diseases through sharing injecting equipment; and premature mortality from overdose, violence, and other causes (Hall, Lynskey, & Degenhardt, 1999b). The major harm associated with the use of heroin in Australia is the risk of fatal and non-fatal overdose (Bammer, Ostini, & Sengoz, 1995; Darke & Ross, 1997a; Darke, Ross, & Hall, 1996a, 1996b; Darke & Zador, 1996; Loxley et al., 1995; Lynskey & Hall, 1998b). The number of fatal opioid overdoses in Australia rose from 6 in 1964 to 600 in 1997, a 55-fold increase in rate when adjusted for growth in popu-lation (Hall et al., 1999b) and dramatic as shown in Figure 3.3. The number increased again in 1998 to 737 deaths (Hall et al., 1999b).

Non-fatal heroin overdose is common among regular heroin users, with recent studies finding that between 45 and 65% of dependent heroin users report a non-fatal overdose at some time in their 10-year histories of use (Darke & Ross, 1997a; Darke et al., 1996a; Gossop, Griffiths, Powis, Williamson, & Strang, 1996).

The typical fatal overdose victim in Australia and most other countries is a single, unemployed male of approximately 30 years, who is a long-term dependent heroin user and was not in treatment at the time of death (Darke & Zador, 1996; Zador, Sunjic, & Darke, 1996). There is a strong association between a fatal and a non-fatal

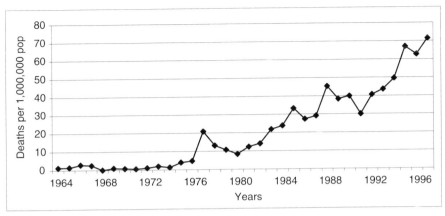

Figure 3.3. Opioid overdose death rate 1964–1997 (rate per million Australian adults 15–44 years).

overdose and the concomitant use of alcohol and benzodiazepines (Darke & Ross, 1997a; Darke et al., 1996a, 1996b; Darke, Ross, Zador, & Sunjic, 2000b; Darke & Zador, 1996; Zador et al., 1996). Contrary to popular conception, fluctuations in heroin purity do not wholly explain the number of overdose fatalities (Darke, Hall, Weatherburn, & Lind, 1999). Variations in the user's opiate tolerance may be more important (Darke, Hall, Kaye, Ross, & DeFluo, 2000a; Tagliaro, De Battisti, Smith, & Marigo, 1998).

Blood-borne viruses (primarily HIV and hepatitis B and C), a major harm to health, are caused by the injection of heroin and other drugs. Studies of injecting drug users (IDU) in Australia have found that the prevalence of hepatitis C infection was 50%, with higher rates among injectors over the age of 25 years, and in persons who have injected for more than two years, and been imprisoned in the previous year. The rate of new hepatitis C infections is estimated at around 15% per year for injecting drug users. Studies report between 30 and 60% of IDU having antibodies to hepatitis B. As with hepatitis C, older users have a higher prevalence of hepatitis B, with rates over 80% among those seeking treatment. The sharing of used injecting equipment appears to have decreased over the preceding decade (Crofts et al., 1993) with the level of sharing remaining at around 15% of users per month.

Studies have repeatedly shown that heroin-dependent individuals have high rates of psychological disorders, with the most common being depression, anxiety disorders, and antisocial personality disorder (Darke & Ross, 1997b; Dinwiddie, Cottler, Compton, & Abdallah, 1996; Kidorf, Hollander, King, & Brooner, 1998). Heroin users are also over-represented among the homeless (Teesson, Hodder, & Buhrich, 2000b).

Controversies on the positive effects of alcohol and cannabis

Over the past decade there has been considerable controversy about the possible health benefits of alcohol and the possible therapeutic uses of cannabis. Many population studies have shown a U-shaped association between the use of alcohol and mortality. In other words, people who drink moderately have a reduced risk of death compared to those who do not drink at all. The risk of death, however, increases if a person drinks heavily. Studies have also demonstrated a reduction in mortality from coronary artery disease with moderate alcohol consumption, but the benefit is not observed with excessive consumption (Thun et al., 1997).

The area is controversial, with the alcohol industry quick to publish the positive effects of alcohol use. Thun et al. (1997) in an excellent study examined both the adverse and beneficial effects of alcohol consumption in 490,000 men and women over 30 years of age, between 1982 and 1991. A slightly reduced overall mortality with moderate alcohol consumption (up to one or two drinks of alcohol daily) was reported, confirming the findings of previous studies. More specifically, rates of death from all cardiovascular diseases combined were 30–40% lower among men and women reporting at least one drink daily than among non-drinkers. However, it is not known how long moderate alcohol consumption must continue for this benefit to occur.

Cannabis has also been the focus of considerable debate. There are a number of medical conditions for which cannabis may be of medical benefit:

- HIV-related wasting and cancer-related wasting
- pain unrelieved by conventional treatment
- neurological disorders including multiple sclerosis, Tourette's syndrome, and motor neurone disease
- nausea and vomiting which, in cancer patients undergoing chemotherapy, does not respond to conventional treatments.

There are two major challenges. First, cannabis is a crude plant product that contains a complex mixture of many chemicals. This makes production of a standard cannabis product difficult as it is not clear which chemicals are responsible for particular therapeutic effects. Cannabis smoke also contains a variety of substances that are dangerous to health. Second, the legal issues present major challenges. Those who are opposed to the medical use of cannabis are concerned about the social implications, particularly the possibility that medical use may promote recreational use.

A number of countries have adopted a compassionate regime so that those suffering from the range of illnesses above can use cannabis without facing criminal sanctions.

Summary

Persons who are dependent on alcohol and other drugs are at high risk of adverse health and other consequences. Among the greatest risks are accidental injury, drowning, car accidents, falls, violence, and overdose death in the case of heroin. Not all drug-dependent persons develop serious health consequences, and there is some controversy as to whether the moderate use of alcohol has positive health benefits in those over 30 years of age.

Theories of addiction: Causes and maintenance of addiction 4

Overview: Theories of addiction

In attempting to explain why people become dependent on drugs, a variety of different approaches have been taken. What follows is a summary of three different areas of explanation. The first concentrates on the neurobiological effects of drugs, and explains drug dependence in biological terms. The second approach is psychological, with explanations concentrating on behavioural models and individual differences. The final approach is sociocultural, with explanations concentrating on the cultural and environmental factors that make drug dependence more likely. As will become clear, there are a variety of approaches to the question of why people become dependent on drugs. These are not mutually exclusive.

Neuroscientific theories

Neuroscientific theories require an understanding of the effects of drugs on the brain, and Box 4.1 outlines the actions of each of the major drug classes. Different drugs clearly have different primary actions on the brain, but two major pathways – the dopamine reward system and the endogenous opioid system – have been implicated as common to most drugs (Koob & LeMoal, 1997; Nutt, 1997).

BOX 4.1 Molecular and cellular sites of drug action

Alcohol

Alcohol has several primary targets of action, and identifying the mechanisms of action has proved to be a difficult task. Acute administration of alcohol leads to increases in inhibitory transmission at gamma-amino-butyric acid (GABA-A) channels, increased serotonin (5HT-3) function, dopamine release and transmission at opiate receptors, and a reduction of excitatory transmission at the NMDA subtype of the glutamate receptor (Altman et al., 1996; Markou, Kosten, & Koob, 1998).

Nicotine

Nicotine is an agonist at the nicotinic receptor – that is, it activates the nicotinic receptor. Nicotinic receptor activation results in increased transmission of a number of neurotransmitters including acetylcholine, norepinephrine, dopamine, serotonin, glutamate, and endorphin (Benowitz, 1998).

Cannabis

The main active ingredient in cannabis is Δ^9-tetrahydrocannabinol (Δ^9-THC), which acts as an agonist at the cannabinoid receptor in the brain. This action results in the prevention of the uptake of dopamine, serotonin, GABA, and norepinephrine (Comings et al., 1997). The cannabinoid (CB1) receptor is most common in the hippocampus, ganglia, and cerebellum (Comings et al., 1997).

Opiates

The brain's endogenous opioid system constitutes peptides including endorphins and enkephalins, which are stored in opiate neurons and released to mediate endogenous opiate actions (Altman et al., 1996; Nutt, 1997).

Opiate drugs act as agonists at three major opiate receptor subtypes: μ (mu), δ (delta), and κ (kappa). The mu receptor appears to be the subtype important for the reinforcing effects of opiate drugs (Altman et al., 1996; Di Chiara & North, 1992). Mu receptors are largely located on cell bodies of dopamine neurons in the ventral tegmental area (VTA), the origin of the mesolimbic dopamine system; and on neurons in the basal forebrain, particularly the nucleus accumbens (Altman et al., 1996; Di Chiara & North, 1992). Delta opiate receptors may be important for the potentiation of the control of reinforcers over behaviour (Altman et al., 1996). There is some evidence that kappa opiate receptors are involved in the aversive effects associated with withdrawal symptoms of opiates (Altman et al., 1996).

Psychomotor Stimulants

Cocaine

Cocaine binds to dopamine, noradrenaline, and serotonin transporters (Altman et al., 1996), but it is thought that cocaine's blockage of dopamine re-uptake is the most important element mediating its reinforcing and psychomotor stimulant effects. This has been supported by recent evidence showing that dopamine D1-like receptors may play an important role in the euphoric and stimulating effects of cocaine. A D1 antagonist significantly attenuated the euphoric and stimulating effects of cocaine, and reduced the desire to take cocaine, among cocaine-dependent persons (Romach et al., 1999).

BOX 4.1   Continued

Amphetamine

Amphetamine acts to increase monoamine release, as well as to increase release of dopamine, with secondary effects occurring in the inhibition of dopamine re-uptake and metabolism (Altman et al., 1996; Stahl, 1996). Similarly to cocaine, the enhanced release and inhibited re-uptake of dopamine is thought to be most important for amphetamine's reinforcing effects (Altman et al., 1996).

Benzodiazepines

Benzodiazepines act by binding with sites on the GABA-A/benzodiazepine receptor (Altman et al., 1996). This results in an increase in chloride conductance through chloride channels, thus enhancing inhibitory transmission. Increased dopamine transmission has been found in the VTA following acute benzodiazepine administration (Altman et al., 1996), but decreased dopamine levels occur in the nucleus accumbens.

Dopamine reward system

The mesolimbic–fronto cortical dopamine system (containing the mesolimbic and mesocortical dopamine systems) is regarded as a critical pathway in brain reward (Nutt, 1997; Wise, 1996). Dopamine has been implicated in the reinforcing effects of alcohol, with alcohol use resulting in the direct stimulation of dopamine and also an indirect increase in dopamine levels (Altman et al., 1996). It is also thought that the behavioural rewards of nicotine, and perhaps the basis of nicotine dependence, are also linked to the release of dopamine in the mesolimbic pathway (Benowitz, 1998; Markou et al., 1998). Following administration of nicotine, increased dopamine is released in rats, and lesions in the mesolimbic dopamine pathway lead to reduced self-administration of nicotine (Altman et al., 1996).

Cannabis was long considered an "atypical" drug, in that it did not interact with the brain's reward system. However, research has revealed that the active component of cannabis, Δ^9-tetrahydrocannabinol (Δ^9-THC), produces enhancement of brain-stimulation reward in rats, at doses within the range of human use (Gardner, 1992). Studies have also revealed cannabinoid receptors in areas associated with brain reward, and that Δ^9-THC increases dopamine levels (Adams & Martin, 1996; Gardner, 1992). This suggests that cannabis does in fact interact with the dopaminergic system. Cocaine's effects have also been related to an increase in dopamine function (Bergman, Kamien, & Spealman, 1990; Caine & Koob, 1994; Spealman, 1990; Spealman, Bargman, Madras, & Melia, 1991).

Endogenous opioid system

There is evidence that the brain's endogenous opioid system may play an important role in drug use and misuse. Exogenous opiates such as heroin, morphine, and codeine act as opiate receptor agonists, and readily cause tolerance and dependence. Adaptation of opiate receptors occurs quite readily after chronic opiate use, as is seen in the need to use larger amounts to achieve pain relief or euphoria. Further, the opiate antagonist naloxone will quickly induce withdrawal symptoms if administered.

Research is increasingly suggesting that the opioid system may be involved in the rewarding effects of other psychoactive substances. One form of therapy for alcohol dependence is the use of the opiate antagonist naltrexone, which has been shown to block the reinforcing properties of alcohol, suggesting that the endogenous opioid system may play an important role in the rewarding effects of alcohol. Recent research suggests that long-term tobacco-smoking may cause changes in the responsivity of the endogenous opioid system, which leads to an increased likelihood of developing nicotine dependence (Krishnan-Sarin, Rosen, & O'Malley, 1999). Research has also found that doses of naloxone reverse the enhancement of brain reward caused by the active component of cannabis, Δ^9-THC (Gardner, 1992).

The dopaminergic and opioid systems have been characterized by some theorists as playing two different functions (Di Chiara & North, 1992). The dopaminergic pathway is associated with the incentive, preparatory aspects of reward, which are experienced as thrill, urgency, or craving. In contrast, the opioid system is associated with the satiation and consummatory aspects of reward, such as rest, blissfulness, and sedation (Di Chiara & North, 1992).

Biological factors

One area of research has concentrated on exploring biological characteristics that underlie drug dependence. These can be grouped into two kinds of explanations; one which examines individual differences in liability to drug dependence because of genetic characteristics, and one which accounts for drug dependence in terms of changes that occur in the brain due to chronic drug administration.

Genetic factors

One hypothesis concerning drug dependence is that people may inherit an increased likelihood (*vulnerability*) of developing dependence on substances. The question of whether or not such vulnerability exists has been examined in the form of numerous family studies, adoption studies, and twin studies.

Family studies of alcohol use disorders suggest that such disorders do cluster in families (Kendler, Davis, & Kessler, 1997; Merikangas, 1990; Merikangas et al., 1998). In a recent study, over one-third (36%) of the relatives of persons with an alcohol use disorder were also diagnosed with an alcohol use disorder (abuse or dependence), compared to 15% of the relatives of controls (Merikangas et al., 1998). This relationship was stronger in a study that examined the rate of alcohol *dependence* among *siblings*: among subjects identified with alcohol dependence, 50% of male siblings met criteria for alcohol dependence, compared to 20% of controls' male siblings; the respective rates for female siblings were 24% and 6% (Bierut et al., 1998). Clearly, alcohol use disorder is likely to occur in more than one family member.

Similar aggregation has been found for other drug use disorders (Bierut et al., 1998; Merikangas et al., 1998). Among persons whose predominant problematic drug was cannabis, 13% of relatives also had a cannabis use disorder, compared to 2.4% of controls' relatives. The comparative rates for opiates were 10% vs. 0.4% and, for cocaine, 7.5% vs. 0.8% (Merikangas et al., 1998).

While these studies suggest that substance use disorders cluster within families, family studies do not allow us to separate the effects of genetic and environmental influences. The clustering may occur simply because the siblings share the same environment rather than any underlying genetic cause. The separate contribution of genes and environment can be teased apart in studies of adopted children and of monozygotic and dizygotic twins.

Adoption studies examine rates of disorder among adoptees, given their biological and adoptive parents' disorder status. This allows evaluation of the effects of genetic (biological parents' status) and environmental (adoptive parents' status) effects on vulnerability to substance use disorders. Research suggests that there is a significant genetic factor that influences adoptees' vulnerability to alcohol use disorders (Bohman, Sigvardsson, & Cloninger, 1981; Cloninger, Bohman, & Sigvardsson, 1981; Goodwin, Schulsinger, Hermansen, Guze, & Winokur, 1973; Heath, 1995).

Researchers have attempted to develop models of vulnerability to substance use disorders, in which vulnerability is the product of genetic and/or environmental factors. Research with twins suggests that there is a significant genetic component (*heritability*) that increases the likelihood of dependence on a range of substances. For example, twin studies have produced estimates of the heritability of alcohol dependence ranging from 39 to 60% of the total variance (Heath, 1995; Kendler et al., 1997; Kendler, Heath, Neale, Kessler, & Eaves, 1992; Kendler, Neale, Heath, Kessler, & Eaves, 1994; Prescott & Kendler, 1999; Prescott, Neale, Corey, & Kendler, 1997; True et al., 1999). Similarly, the heritability of smoking persistence has been estimated at 53% (Heath & Martin, 1993), and that for nicotine dependence between 60 and 70% (Kendler et al., 1999a; True et al., 1999). Research examining dependence on other drugs has revealed significant heritability estimates for cannabis dependence (Kendler & Prescott, 1998b; Tsuang et al., 1998) and dependence on heroin, sedatives, and stimulants (Kendler & Prescott, 1998b; Tsuang et al., 1996, 1998).

These findings suggest a further issue: Do persons have a vulnerability towards one specific drug, or is there a more general vulnerability to a class of drugs or, indeed, to any psychoactive substance? In one discussion of this question, researchers concluded: "There is no definitive evidence indicating that individuals who habitually and preferentially use one substance are fundamentally different from those who use another" (Tarter & Mezzich, 1992). A recent study found that among the relatives of persons with substance use disorders, rates of *all* substance use disorders were higher than those among the relatives of controls (Merikangas et al., 1998).

Other recent research involving male twins has also examined the issue of a common genetic vulnerability to substance misuse (True et al., 1999; Tsuang et al., 1998). One of these studies examined the genetic and environmental contributions to illicit substance abuse and dependence (cannabis, stimulants, sedatives, opiates, and psychedelics) (Tsuang et al., 1998). It found that there was a significant common genetic component (16% of the variance for heroin, 22% for cannabis, stimulants, sedatives, and 26% for psychedelics). Around one-third of the variance in this common vulnerability was caused by genetic effects. A similar analysis of alcohol and nicotine dependence (True et al., 1999) suggested that there was a significant common genetic vulnerability ($r = 0.68$) to both nicotine and alcohol dependence among male twins, with 26% of the total variance in the risk for alcohol dependence shared with genetic risk of nicotine dependence.

Genetic characteristics

The exact nature of these genetic vulnerabilities has been the subject of increasing research. Thus far, no single candidate genes have been discovered that are directly related to drug abuse (Altman et al., 1996); it is likely that these influences may involve multiple genes or incomplete expression of several major genes (Kendler, 1999; Schuckit, 1999). For example, there is recent evidence to suggest a relationship between tobacco-smoking and genes involved in dopamine regulation (Lerman et al., 1999; Pomerleau & Kardia, 1999; Sabol et al., 1999). Research examining the gene for the brain's cannabinoid system (CNR1) found that variants of the CNR1 gene were associated with cannabis, cocaine, and heroin dependence (Comings et al., 1997).

Neuroadaptation

One theory of drug dependence is based on the concept of neuroadaptation (Koob & LeMoal, 1997). Neuroadaptation refers to changes in the brain that occur to oppose a drug's acute actions after repeated drug administration. This may be of two types: *within-system adaptations*, where the changes occur at the site of the drug's action, and *between-system adaptations*, which are changes in different mechanisms that are triggered by the drug's action. When drugs are repeatedly administered, changes occur in the chemistry of the brain to oppose the drug's effects. When this drug use is discontinued, the adaptations are no longer opposed; the brain's homeostasis is disrupted (Koob & LeMoal, 1997).

Essentially, this hypothesis argues that tolerance to the effects of a drug and withdrawal when drug use stops are both the result of neuroadaptation (Koob, Caine, Parsons, Markou, & Weiss, 1997). Animal models have shown that stressful stimuli activate the dopamine reward system, so vulnerability to relapse from abstinence is hypothesized to occur. As a result, drug use continues in an attempt to avoid the symptoms that follow if drug use stops (Koob & LeMoal, 1997).

While, traditionally, conceptualizations of drug dependence focused on physical withdrawal symptoms, more recent formulations have begun to concentrate on the presence of more motivational symptoms, such as dysphoria, depression, irritability, and anxiety. It has been hypothesized that these negative motivational symptoms are manifestations of neurobiological changes, and that these changes signal "not only . . . the beginning of the development of dependence, but may also contribute to vulnerability to relapse and may also have motivational significance" (Koob et al., 1997, p. 53). This approach hypothesizes that, after chronic drug use, changes occur in the dopamine reward system and the endogenous opioid system.

Psychological theories

Psychological approaches to the explanation of drug dependence have often been based on concepts that are common to those of other syndromes of behaviour involving compulsive or impulsive behaviours, such as obsessive–compulsive disorder or gambling (Miller, 1980). In particular, emphasis is given to the fact that there is impaired control over use and continued use despite usage problems. There are a variety of psychological approaches to the explanation of drug dependence, including emphasis on learning and conditioning (behavioural models), cognitive theories, pre-existing behavioural tendencies (personality theories), and models of rational choice.

Behavioural theories

Behaviourist models of addiction focus on directly observable behaviour. One group concentrates on the fact that behaviour is maintained (or made more likely) by the consequences (reinforcers) of such behaviour (West, 1989). Drug self-administration is then an example of *instrumental behaviour* because the activities of persons (or animals in an experiment) are instrumental in obtaining the consequences (the drug's effects).

Research with animal subjects has shown that when drugs are available, drug-naive animals will self-administer them, often to excess (Institute of Medicine, 1996). This observation has led to the development of the *drug self-administration model*. Drugs might be reinforcing in two general ways: through the direct effects of drugs on some sort of reinforcement system in the brain; or through its effects on other reinforcers (such as social or sexual reinforcers) or behavioural effects (such as increased attention) (Altman et al., 1996).

Research with animals has shown that they will self-administer most drugs (except LSD and Δ^9-THC) in instrumental paradigms

(Altman et al., 1996), and this finding has been replicated with many species of animal and a variety of routes of administration (Institute of Medicine, 1996).

In using these animal research models, it has been possible to control the history of use (learning) and current environmental conditions of use (cues). As a result, it has been shown that both of these factors are important in the development of persistent use or abuse of drugs (Barrett & Witkin, 1986).

These findings point to another group of behaviourist theories, which focus on *classical conditioning* (Greeley & Westbrook, 1991; Heather & Greeley, 1990) and this sort of learning has been found to play an important part in the development and maintenance of addictive behaviours. *Cue exposure theory* is based on classical conditioning theory, and argues that cues are important in the development and maintenance of addictive behaviour (Drummond, Tiffany, Glautier, & Remington, 1995; Heather & Greeley, 1990). A cue that has previously been present when drugs were administered will be more likely to elicit a conditioned response (cue reactivity). This is thought to underlie craving, and may explain why someone who was dependent on a substance but has been abstinent for some time experiences strong cravings (Heather & Greeley, 1990).

The number of cues that may be associated with addictive behaviours is potentially infinite. Exteroceptive cues occur before the use of a drug, and may include the smell of an alcoholic drink, the sight of a needle, or may even constitute the time of day when drugs are typically taken. Interoceptive cues include such things as the effects of a drug on the brain's receptors, mood cues such as depressed affect (Greeley, Swift, & Heather, 1992), or cognitions such as beliefs about drug effects (Drummond et al., 1995).

The response to these cues may be autonomic, behavioural, or symbolic-expressive (Drummond et al., 1995). Autonomic responses that have been observed in cue exposure experiments include changes in heart rate, temperature, and salivation; symbolic-expressive responses that have been observed include self-reported drug-craving and urges to use drugs; and behavioural responses include an increased likelihood to use drugs.

Cognitive theories

There are a number of theories that explain drug dependence in terms of cognitive constructs. One theory proposes that *self-regulation* is an important factor in the development of drug use problems. Self-regulation has been described as taking "planful action designed to change the course of one's behaviour" (Miller & Brown, 1991), the "executive (i.e. non-automatic) capacity to plan, guide and monitor one's behaviour flexibly, according to changing circumstances" (Diaz & Fruhauf, 1991). Self-regulation involves planning, taking into account social and physical factors as well as one's own goals, and acting appropriately. Addictive behaviours are seen as the result of having an excessive reliance on external structures – in the case of drug dependence, excessive reliance on substance use – to maintain a physical and psychological balance.

Personality theories

Some theorists argue that certain people are more prone to addiction through a so-called "addictive personality". Hans Eysenck has discussed this in terms of a *psychological resource model*, whereby the habit of drug-taking is developed because the drug used fulfils a certain purpose that is related to the individual's personality profile (Eysenck, 1997). For such people, drug-taking behaviour – or, more specifically, "addiction" – holds benefits even though there are negative consequences that occur after some time.

According to Eysenck, there are three major and independent personality dimensions: P (psychoticism), N (neuroticism), and E (extraversion) (Eysenck & Eysenck, 1985). The psychoticism dimension refers to an underlying propensity to functional psychosis, which lies along a continuum from "altruistic" to "schizophrenic" (Eysenck, 1997). Some of the characteristic traits of this dimension are aggression, coldness, egocentricity, impersonality, and impulsivity. The neuroticism dimension refers to a propensity towards emotional lability: some of the traits of neuroticism are moodiness, irritability, and anxiety. Genetic factors are theorized to play an important role in determining these personality dimensions; indeed, studies have shown that the major personality dimensions have high heritability (Eley & Plomin, 1997; Eysenck, 1997).

There has been extensive examination of the relationship between drug dependence and these personality dimensions. Research examining the link between E and drug dependence has revealed inconsistent findings; in a review of research on this topic, 10 studies found a negative relationship, 2 found a positive correlation, and 12 found no significant relationship (Francis, 1996). In contrast, there has been considerable research suggesting that persons with dependence on a range of substances – alcohol, heroin, benzodiazepines, nicotine – have higher than normal N and P scores (Francis, 1996).

This research suggests that persons who are more moody, irritable, and anxious (high N scores), and those who are more impulsive and aggressive (high P scores), are also more likely to have substance use problems. However, on the basis of correlational studies such as those above, it is difficult to make any statements about the nature of the relationship between these and substance use problems. It may be the case, for example, that persons who develop problematic drug use become more irritable, moody, or aggressive as a result of changes that occur due to their drug use. Furthermore, research examining the genetic contributions to personality suggests that dimensions such as N may indicate vulnerability to psychopathology *in general*, not simply a tendency to have an "addictive personality" per se.

Other research, conducted with longitudinal studies of children, has examined personality attributes that predict substance use at a later stage and has found that, in general, adolescents who are more rebellious and have less conventional attitudes are more likely to drink, smoke, and use illicit drugs (Institute of Medicine, 1996).

Rational choice theories

One group of theories examines the problem of why people voluntarily engage in self-destructive behaviour (Elster & Skog, 1999). One of the central elements of drug dependence is the fact that the individuals have impaired control over their use of the substance. This may manifest itself in continued use despite a wish to reduce or stop use of the drug, to use greater amounts of the drug than intended, or to use the drug for longer periods than intended (American Psychiatric Association, 1994). This difficulty may be greater in certain contexts – for example, if an alcohol-dependent person has not had a drink for some time and walks past a bar.

Some would argue that this represents a form of "weakness of will": that addiction is an example of behaving "against one's own better judgement" (Davidson, 1985; Pears, 1984). For such theorists, drug-dependent persons have a choice of two options, both of which may be evaluated in terms of their future consequences. They realize that one option is superior, yet choose the other; for instance, an individual may have made the decision to stop drinking and yet accept a drink from someone even though the individual knows, at that particular time, that he or she should not.

As Elster and Skog (1999) point out, the problem with this approach is that it is difficult to know whether such a person knew *at the time of acceptance* that choosing the drink was the less preferred option. The person may have made this considered decision before the party, and regretted accepting the drink after the party, but it is difficult to ascertain whether he or she thought so at the time of accepting the drink.

In contrast, some theorists argue that drug-dependent persons *do* make rational choices in their continued use of drugs. The aim of these theories is to explain how rational people can become "knowingly trapped in a consumption pattern . . . and . . . once they realise that their current lifestyle is actually suboptimal (i.e. not the best thing, all things considered), still continue to act the same way" (Skog, 1999).

A number of attempts to explain this paradox have centred on people's ability to weigh present and future benefits – in other words, their ability to consider the immediate rewards associated with drug use, weighed against the longer-term benefits of abstention (Ainslie, 1992; Becker & Murphy, 1988; Herrnstein & Prelec, 1992). One approach has been to argue that people have a limited ability to consider future benefits – "cognitive myopia" (Herrnstein & Prelec, 1992); hence, the choice to use drugs at one particular time is rational, given the considered options. Two other approaches have argued that while people are able to consider a range of future benefits, present and future benefits are differentially weighted, with greater weight given to the present (Ainslie, 1992; Becker & Murphy, 1988).

Contextual factors

There are a number of social and environmental factors that have been strongly related to substance use and substance use disorders. These are in keeping with the findings of twin studies, which show that while there is a strong genetic component to vulnerability to drug dependence, there is also a substantial environmental component (Kendler & Gardner, 1998; Kendler, Karkowski, & Prescott, 1999b; Kendler & Prescott, 1998a). A range of these factors are outlined below.

There is much evidence to suggest that people with antisocial behaviour are more likely to have or develop substance use problems. Adolescents with conduct disorders are significantly more likely to develop substance use disorders than those without such conduct problems (Cicchetti & Rogosch, 1999; Gittelman, Mannuzza, Shenker, & Bonagura, 1985). In general, it appears that the earlier, more varied and more serious a child's antisocial behaviour, the more likely will it be continued into adulthood, with substance misuse considered as one of these antisocial behaviours (Costello, Erkanli, Federman, & Angold, 1999; Robins, 1978). Furthermore, children or young people with anxiety or depressive symptoms are more likely to begin substance use at an earlier age, and to develop substance use problems (Cicchetti & Rogosch, 1999; Costello et al., 1999; Henry et al., 1993; Loeber, Southamer-Lober, & White, 1999).

The peer environment also has a large influence on the drug-taking behaviour of individuals. Drug use usually begins with peers, and peer attitudes to drug use have been shown to be highly predictive of adolescent drug use (Fergusson & Horwood, 1997; Hoefler et al., 1999; Newcomb, Maddahian, & Bentler, 1986) perhaps because those who use drugs are more likely to choose to spend time with peers who also use drugs. There is, however, no evidence concerning the influence of peers on the development or maintenance of drug *dependence* (Institute of Medicine, 1996).

Families also have a strong effect on the likelihood that people will develop substance use problems (Hawkins, Catalano, & Miller, 1992; Lynskey & Hall, 1998a) and this may occur in a number of ways. First, modelling of substance use by parents and other family members has been shown to affect the chances of the substance use behaviour of adolescents. For example, parents' drug use has been associated with the initiation and frequency of alcohol and cannabis use (Hawkins et al., 1992), while older brothers' drug use and attitudes towards drug use have been associated with younger brothers' drug use (Brook, Whiteman, Gordon, & Brook, 1988). Second, there is evidence that if parents hold permissive attitudes towards the use of drugs by their children, their children will be more likely to use drugs (Hawkins et al., 1992). Third, the nature of family relationships has an effect on the likelihood that adolescents will develop problematic drug use. The risk of substance misuse is higher if there is family discord, poor or inconsistent behavioural management techniques by parents, or low levels of bonding within the family (Hawkins et al., 1992).

The sociocultural background of a person will also affect the likelihood that he or she will develop substance use problems; for example, people who come from lower socioeconomic backgrounds are more likely to have problematic use of a range of drugs (Anthony,

Warner, & Kessler, 1994; Hall, Johnston, & Donnelly, 1999a). Those who have completed fewer years of education, or who have performed poorly in school, are also much more likely to have problematic substance use. Also, people who have grown up in an area in which there are high rates of crime, where drugs are readily available, and who have associated with delinquent peers, are much more likely to have drug misuse problems (Institute of Medicine, 1996).

Summary

The neurochemistry of chronic drug use is being more clearly described and understood. It appears that key pathways in the brain are involved in substance use and dependence, and research has revealed that changes in the brain's balance and neurotransmitter function occur after chronic drug use. So why do some people become dependent on drugs? Genetic factors do appear to play a part. Significant genetic components have been found to play a part in dependence on many of the most commonly used licit and illicit substances, suggesting that some persons are more vulnerable than others to developing drug use problems. There is also consistent evidence that certain environmental factors will increase the likelihood of problematic substance use, such as economic disadvantage, family conflict, modelling of drug use, or parents' permissive attitudes towards drug use, as well as conduct and emotional problems at an early age.

Psychological approaches to the issue of substance dependence have attempted to explain some of the behavioural and cognitive phenomena thought to underlie problematic substance use. Some theories – such as those proposing a personality type more disposed to addiction, or those characterizing the "rational" addict – have less importance for clinicians. However, learning theories hold considerable importance: they can be empirically tested, and supporting evidence suggests that learning plays an important role in the development and maintenance of substance use problems. In the same way, learning may be used to overcome these problems.

Clearly, there have been a number of approaches to explain why some people become dependent on psychoactive substances. Each level of explanation – genetic, psychological, or sociocultural – has been supported by empirical research, but these different levels remain to be integrated into a more comprehensive model of addiction.

Currently, the biopsychosocial model of the causes of addictive behaviours forms the basis of most treatment responses to addictions (Marlatt & VandenBos, 1997). In contrast to the disease model, the biopsychosocial model sees "addiction" as a complex behaviour pattern having biological, psychological, sociological, and behavioural components. These include the subjective experience of craving, short-term gratification at the risk of longer-term harm, and rapid change in physical and psychological states. Addictive behaviour is distinguished from other problem behaviours by the individual's overwhelming, pathological involvement in drug use, intense desire to continue using the drugs, and lack of control over his or her drug use. This theory provides the principles for the treatment responses to addiction outlined in the next sections of this book.

Alcohol 5

Introduction

Alcohol dependence is one of the most prevalent disorders diagnosed in community surveys of mental disorders, and many people with this disorder have comorbid anxiety and depressive disorders. *Alcohol use disorders* (which include abuse and dependence) typically involve impaired control over the use of alcohol. Obtaining, using, and recovering from alcohol consumes a disproportionate amount of the user's time, and the user continues to drink alcohol in the face of problems that the user knows to be caused by it. Alcohol abusers typically become tolerant to the effects of alcohol, requiring larger doses to achieve the desired psychological effect, and abrupt cessation of use often produces a withdrawal syndrome. Many alcohol abusers experience other psychological and physical health problems, and their alcohol use often adversely affects the lives of their spouses, children, and other family members, friends, and workmates.

This chapter reviews the research literature on effective evidence-based interventions for alcohol abuse, dependence, and excessive drinking.

Assessment

Assessment is an important first stage in interventions and treatments for addictions, including alcohol, and involves a review of the quantity of substance used and the health and social consequences. Two important roles of assessment are to provide feedback to the individual on his or her drug use and to develop a rapport between the therapist and the individual. The aim of assessment is to:

- identify why the individual continues to take a drug that is causing harm
- identify the main diagnosis and any other comorbid disorders or problems (identify harms)
- highlight the areas that require intervention (e.g., alcohol consumption) to enable goals to be set and a management plan to be devised
- identify a baseline against which improvement or deterioration can be measured.

Assessment measures for alcohol have proliferated. Assessment can range from brief screening interviews by general health care workers, which may lead to early intervention, to in-depth assessment of a broad range of psychosocial functions in order to formulate and evaluate treatment.

Standardized methods of screening for excessive drinking include the use of clinical examinations, testing for biological markers, and the use of standardardized questionnaires. Standard clinical examinations, which involve identifying physical signs of excessive alcohol consumption, such as bloodshot eyes and coating of the tongue, have been found to be accurate for detecting alcohol dependence but are not sensitive enough for detecting signs of hazardous, non-dependent drinking (Mattick & Jarvis, 1993). The most widely used biological marker for alcohol abuse is serum gamma glutamyltransferase (GGT), a liver enzyme that is elevated in 55–80% of people with alcohol disorders.

A range of standard questionnaires have been designed to screen for alcohol abuse. The 24-item Michigan Alcoholism Screening Test (MAST; Selzer, 1971), its shortened 13-item version, and the 4-item CAGE (Mayfield, McLeod, & Hall, 1974) have been shown to be valid in identifying alcohol dependence in males, but their ability to detect hazardous drinking in females has not been established (Cherpitel, 1995). The TWEAK is a 5-item version of CAGE (Russell & Bigler, 1979).

A more recently developed measure is the Alcohol Use Disorders Identification Test (AUDIT; Table 5.1). The AUDIT was developed as part of a World Health Organization study of brief alcohol interventions and was based on research carried out in six countries. It comprises 10 questions assessing alcohol consumption, drinking behaviour, and alcohol-related problems during the past year and has been shown to validly detect at-risk drinking behaviour cross-nationally (Saunders, Aasland, Babor, delaFuente, & Grant, 1993).

TABLE 5.1

Alcohol Use Disorders Identification Test (AUDIT)

Circle the number that comes closest to your answer.

1. How often do you have a drink containing alcohol?

   (0) Never   (1) Monthly or less   (2) Two to four times a month   (3) Two to three times a week   (4) Four or more times a week

2. How many drinks containing alcohol do you have on a typical day when you are drinking?

   (0) 1 or 2   (1) 3 or 4   (2) 5 or 6   (3) 7 to 9   (4) 10 or more

3. How often do you have six or more drinks on one occasion?

   (0) Never   (1) Less than monthly   (2) Monthly   (3) Weekly   (4) Daily or almost daily

4. How often during the last year have you found that you were not able to stop drinking once you had started?

   (0) Never   (1) Less than monthly   (2) Monthly   (3) Weekly   (4) Daily or almost daily

5. How often during the last year have you failed to do what was normally expected from you because of drinking?

   (0) Never   (1) Less than monthly   (2) Monthly   (3) Weekly   (4) Daily or almost daily

6. How often during the last year have you needed a first drink in the morning to get yourself going after a heavy drinking session?

   (0) Never   (1) Less than monthly   (2) Monthly   (3) Weekly   (4) Daily or almost daily

7. How often during the last year have you had a feeling of guilt or remorse after drinking?

   (0) Never   (1) Less than monthly   (2) Monthly   (3) Weekly   (4) Daily or almost daily

8. How often during the last year have you been unable to remember what happened the night before because you had been drinking?

   (0) Never   (1) Less than monthly   (2) Monthly   (3) Weekly   (4) Daily or almost daily

9. Have you or someone else been injured as a result of your drinking?

   (0) No   (2) Yes, but not in the last year   (4) Yes, during the last year

10. Has a relative or friend or a doctor or other health worker been concerned about your drinking or suggested you cut down?

    (0) No   (2) Yes, but not in the last year   (4) Yes, during the last year

Subsequent research (Conigrave, Hall, & Saunders, 1995) has found that scores on the AUDIT were predictive of a range of alcohol-related problems over a three-year period. Higher AUDIT scores were associated with increasingly severe alcohol problems, which ranged from social disruption to liver disease. Scores of 8 or above (maximum 40) are indicative of problem drinking.

Measures to assess the severity of dependence have been developed in both alcohol and other drug studies. One of the most widely used instruments is the Severity of Alcohol Dependence Questionnaire (SADQ; Stockwell, Sitharthan, McGrath, & Lang, 1994). This 20-item instrument (with a maximum score of 60) has excellent psychometric properties and emphasizes aspects of physical dependence. Scores lower than or equal to 20 indicate low dependence; scores between 21 and 30 indicate moderate dependence; and a score of 30 indicates severe dependence (Stockwell, Murphy, & Hodgson, 1983).

The Short Alcohol Dependence Data Questionnaire (SADDQ; Raistrick, Dunbar, & Davidson, 1983) is similar to the SADQ, but has less focus on physical aspects of alcohol dependence, such as withdrawal symptoms, and more emphasis on psychological elements of dependence, such as behavioural and subjective manifestations. The 24-item Alcohol Dependence Scale (ADS; Skinner & Horn, 1984) is a widely used questionnaire with good reliability and validity.

Self-efficacy relates to an individual's confidence in being able to drink moderately and has been recognized as an important therapeutic construct in alcohol treatment. The Controlled Drinking Situational Confidence Questionnaire (Sitharthan & Kavanagh, 1991) provides a very useful measure of self-efficacy, asking the client to consider his or her confidence in being able to drink moderately, rather than avoiding alcohol altogether.

Physical well-being – as indicated by liver function, blood pressure, withdrawal symptoms, and organic brain damage – should be included in the overall assessment, and the results may prove useful in counselling against continued hazardous drinking.

Cognitive dysfunction should also be assessed by neuropsychological tests. Excessive tremor in the hands and fingers (and even the tongue), staggering gait, and numbness in the fingers and toes also indicate damage to the central nervous system, and such signs should be carefully checked, especially in severe long-term drinkers. The issue will often arise as to whether an individual with an alcohol problem is suffering from brain damage. The diagnosis of lesser degrees of damage is often quite difficult, but one of the most common presentations is alcohol dementia. The individual with alcohol dementia will typically give a history of many years of drinking and may present as the example below:

> A young man, aged 30 years, had been drinking heavily for five years. He reported that his wife complained about his irritability and impaired concentration. His performance as a store manager had recently been reviewed and his boss's appraisal was that his work performance was deteriorating.

Comorbid psychiatric conditions such as depression have been found to influence treatment outcome in addiction. Brief screening measures such as the Beck Depression Inventory (BDI; Beck & Steer, 1987), the Beck Anxiety Inventory (BAI; Beck & Steer, 1990), and the SCL-90 (Derogatis, 1983) can be used to screen for comorbid psychiatric conditions.

> A single woman, aged 25 years, had been drinking excessively for five years. She attended her general practitioner's surgery complaining that she was unable to get out of bed in the morning and felt that she was no good and that the world might as well be rid of her.

The clinician should not only assess her alcohol use but also the severity of her symptoms of depression. Prescribing antidepressants while an individual is drinking heavily is not desirable.

Family issues may have an important bearing on treatment compliance and outcome. Such factors include how the individual's drinking affects family relations, the quality of family relations in general, the presence of violence and abuse, and the commitment of the family to the rehabilitation of the individual. The Alcohol Problems Questionnaire provides an appraisal of family, occupational, and global alcohol-related problems (Williams & Drummond, 1994).

Interventions

Public health interventions

Not all problems with alcohol require individual treatment, and some alcohol problems in the community may be better modified in other ways. Public health policies that reduce the availability and increase the price of alcohol may also reduce the prevalence of alcohol abuse and dependence. Public education about the risks of alcohol dependence may prevent the more prevalent and less severe alcohol use disorders, while advice on self-help strategies may obviate the need for professional assistance in a substantial proportion of cases.

A major development in the prevention of alcoholism and alcohol-related health problems has been the adoption of a public health perspective that shifts attention away from an exclusive focus on the dependent alcohol user to consider the full spectrum of problems caused by alcohol (e.g., road traffic accidents, lost productivity, violence, and diseases such as cancer, liver cirrhosis, brain damage, and heart disease) (Edwards et al., 1994). An important consequence of this perspective is that the prevalence of alcohol-related problems in the community can best be reduced by decreasing the alcohol consumption of a much larger proportion of the population than the minority of "alcoholics". Alcohol sales, therefore, provide a relatively good indicator of the alcohol consumption of the community and a measure of the need for public health responses to alcohol use.

A public health approach to alcohol-related harm adopts a broader conception of the causes of alcohol-related problems. While more traditional approaches have focused on the characteristics that pre-dispose some drinkers to develop alcoholism, the public health approach emphasizes the characteristics of the physical and social environment that encourage hazardous drinking. This is taken to include the advertising and promotion of alcohol, and the community's tolerance of the ready availability of alcohol at compara-tively low prices (Edwards et al., 1994; Walsh & Hingson, 1987).

Some proposals for decreasing population alcohol consumption are: laws and regulations that aim to reduce the availability of alcohol (e.g., licensing regulations that restrict trading hours for liquor out-lets, and the enforcement of laws on under-age drinking); measures that increase the price of alcohol to reduce consumption (e.g., increased taxes levied on the alcohol content of beverages); and regulations to control the promotion of alcohol (Walsh & Hingson, 1987).

The lack of popular and political support for policies that increase the price of alcohol or reduce its availability (Flaherty, Homel, & Hall, 1991) has encouraged a search for other approaches to reduce the public health impact of alcohol use. Foremost among these has been public education of drinkers about the risks of alcohol use. This has been especially prominent in Australia where a combination of education about the maximum number of standard drinks that can be consumed before driving and random breath testing have reduced overall road fatalities and the proportion of fatalities in which the driver had a blood alcohol level above the prescribed level (0.05%). These campaigns enjoy widespread public support and have probably also helped to reduce consumption by providing an excuse for drinkers to moderate their consumption (Homel, 1989).

Brief interventions

Persons who present for medical treatment can be screened for hazardous alcohol use and alcohol-related problems, and those identified as drinking at hazardous levels can be advised to reduce or stop consumption and be given simple ways to achieve these goals (Heather & Tebbutt, 1989). Babor (1994) describes a typical brief intervention as consisting of structured therapy of short duration (5–30 minutes), which is offered to help the individual to cease or reduce drinking or drug-taking. Research has shown that screening and brief advice for excessive alcohol consumption in general practice and hospital settings reduces consumption and the problems caused by alcohol (Chick, Lloyd, & Crombie, 1985; Elvy, Wells, & Baird, 1988; Fleming, 1993; WHO Brief Intervention Study Group, 1996b; Wilk, Jensen, & Havighurst, 1997). Given that considerable costs are involved in providing conventional alcohol treatment (Holder & Blose, 1986; Holder & Schachman, 1987), there is also a good economic argument for brief intervention.

Brief interventions were first promoted in their present form by early researchers in the tobacco-smoking cessation field (Russell & Bigler, 1979). They found that a five-minute opportunistic intervention by a general practitioner, when delivered to thousands of patients who had come to consult about another health matter, had a larger impact on quit rates in the community than intensive interventions delivered to a select few. Heather and colleagues, in a study of self-managed change in the Scottish city of Dundee, found encouraging outcomes in problem drinkers who received a self-help booklet in the post (Heather, 1995a). Further work by Heather found that interventions ranging from five minutes to one hour, delivered either opportunistically or on request, yielded strong outcomes among problem drinkers with mild dependence. This included occasional binge drinkers, as well as steady drinkers who wanted help to reduce their intake. The interventions included: information on safe drinking limits; information about the harmful effects of alcohol; suggestions on useful techniques to cut down; and advice on how to self-monitor the daily alcohol intake.

With results regarding the efficacy of brief interventions in mind, Miller and Marlatt (1984) in the USA developed a Comprehensive Drinker's Profile (CDP). This allowed a therapist to provide a standardized assessment, with appropriate feedback about the likely harm arising from the client's drinking, and put the client in a position to decide what to do about the problem. The CDP is designed to boost client motivation to make changes, and is therefore a particularly effective form of brief intervention.

The WHO Brief Intervention Study Group (1996a) conducted a cross-national, randomized clinical trial comparing a no-treatment control condition with two treatment conditions: 5 minutes of advice or 20 minutes of brief counselling. The initial sample consisted of 1,260 men and 399 women with no history of alcohol dependence who were identified as being at risk of alcohol-related problems. The sample was taken from Australia, Bulgaria, Kenya, Mexico, Norway, and the USA. Subjects were followed up 9 months later; 75% of the sample were interviewed at follow-up and it was assumed for purposes of analysis that there was no change in the drinking behaviour of those not available for follow-up.

Significant improvements were found for males in both treatment groups compared with the control group, but there was no difference between the two treatments. Overall treatment led to a 17% reduction in average daily consumption and a 10% reduction in intensity of drinking and this was consistent across the eight countries. These findings were not due to a few patients achieving abstinence but were distributed across many patients who reduced their drinking by small but meaningful amounts, indicating that moderate drinking can be achieved by a substantial proportion of heavy drinkers. This study reinforces the notion that screening and brief interventions should be conducted in primary health care settings as an efficient way of reducing the negative impact of excessive alcohol use.

In project TrEAT (Trial for Early Alcohol Treatment; Fleming, Barry, Manwell, Johnson, & London, 1997), the first large-scale brief intervention conducted in community-based primary care practices in the USA, 17,695 patients were screened at 17 intervention clinics. Screening took about 30 minutes and was conducted by a trained researcher. Of these patients, 2,925 screened positive and 1,705 (58%) completed a further interview to assess eligibility for the study. Of the 852 patients that were deemed eligible, 774 were randomly assigned to treatment and control conditions and 723 of these were followed up at 12 months. Those lost to follow-up were considered not to have altered their drinking behaviour over the period of the study.

The treatment group was given a workbook that contained feed-back about current health behaviours, a review of the prevalence of problem drinking, associated risks, a list of drinking cues, a drinking agreement in the form of a prescription, and diary cards. Brief intervention and reinforcement consisted of two 15-minute sessions, 1 month apart, with a physician; then a follow-up call from a nurse 2 weeks after each meeting. The control group was given a booklet on general health issues and followed up at 6 and 12 months. Outcome measures were average drinks per week, binge-drinking, and excessive drinking, as well as emergency department visits and hospital days. Both groups showed improvement and there were greater improvements in the experimental condition than in the controls for both sexes when measured by consumption in the past 7 days, episodes of binge-drinking during the past month, and frequency of excessive drinking. There was no clear evidence of decreased use of health care services for either group.

The research on brief interventions has found that they are more effective than no treatment, and often as effective as more intensive interventions (Mattick & Jarvis, 1993). Experts in the field emphasize that the value of intensive interventions for particular patients in specific contexts should not be dismissed out of hand (Mattick & Jarvis, 1993). More research is needed that takes adequate account of the factors confounding the research to date.

Results are restricted by a lack of generalizability to the broad drinking population (Drummond, 1997; Heather, 1995b). Subjects treated with brief interventions in studies of their effectiveness tend to have a good prognosis – that is, they are older and more moderate drinkers with no comorbid conditions. Furthermore, findings of effectiveness have not been consistently replicated in female drinkers.

Apart from these specific criticisms of the research on brief interventions, more general issues have also been raised by expert reviewers. Throughout the literature, brief interventions are referred to as one intervention, when in fact they represent a range of treat-ments varying in length and content. According to Heather (1995b), it is not known which brief interventions are effective for which types of patients or in which circumstances. Hence it is misleading to refer to the effectiveness of brief interventions as such, unless these variables are more clearly specified.

Despite these criticisms of the research to date, the experts are optimistic that further research is likely to lead to more appropriate and cost-effective applications of brief interventions in treating alcohol abuse problems in the community (Rollnick, Butler, & Hodgson, 1997).

Treatment goal: Abstinence or moderation

The controlled drinking debate is one of the great debates in the addictions. Research suggests that less dependent drinkers may achieve controlled drinking, whereas severely dependent drinkers should aim at abstinence (Mattick & Jarvis, 1993). Sobell and Sobell (1995b) argue similarly that from the available research, irrespective of the stated treatment goals or the amount of drinking skills training, the most likely positive outcome of treatment for low dependence drinkers is controlled drinking while, for high dependence drinkers, it is abstinence. They point out that background factors, such as lack of social support and poor vocational history, may be more important in deciding treatment aims than level of dependence.

There has been much interest and controversy about moderation as a legitimate treatment goal for alcohol dependence, especially as it is in direct conflict with the tenets of Alcoholics Anonymous (AA) that holds that no "alcoholic" is able to moderate his or her consumption of alcohol for any length of time. Abstinence, according to AA, is the only defensible and achievable goal for persons who are alcohol dependent.

The earliest work in this area was conducted by Davies (1962) working with hospitalized patients in the UK. He found in a 10-year follow-up that a substantial proportion of the cohort had returned to drinking moderately. Sobell and Sobell followed this preliminary research with one of the first randomized controlled trials in the alcohol treatment literature (Sobell & Sobell, 1995a). They found that problem drinkers were just as likely to master controlled drinking as those who were trained in abstinence techniques. However, a backlash occurred against the Sobells when a television programme ran a story suggesting that several members of the controlled drinking group had died, presumably from the effects of drinking. While four members of the moderate drinking group had indeed died, five of the abstinence-treated group had died, and these were more likely to have died of the effects of harmful drinking.

More recent research suggests that those who have a dependence on alcohol that is mild to moderate (as measured by the Severity of Alcohol Dependence Questionnaire), have good means of social support, and have a stable psychosocial profile are more likely to succeed with controlled drinking (Heather & Robertson, 1983). Indeed, this is true also for those who receive abstinence-oriented treatment. Perhaps the foremost indicator of outcome of a controlled drinking intervention is the individual's desire to become a safe drinker.

Detoxification

Detoxification is the removal of a drug from the body. It involves assisting the individual to recover from the effects of chronic intoxication so that withdrawal symptoms are minimized. The severity of alcohol withdrawal depends on such factors as level and duration of use, accompanying drug use, the general health and nutritional state of the person, and the detoxification setting (Mattick & Jarvis, 1993). Withdrawal or detoxification from alcohol can be life threatening.

Detoxification itself can be medicated or unmedicated. Unmedicated withdrawal involves withdrawing from alcohol without drugs to assist the process. Medicated withdrawal involves substitution for uncontrolled alcohol use by a controlled drug that has a similar action to the abused drug. In the case of alcohol, benzodiazapines such as diazepam, chlordiazapoxide, and chlormethiazole may be used (Mayo-Smith, 1997).

Detoxification can be home-based or inpatient. Where a person is considered likely to suffer mild to moderate withdrawal, is not in need of sedative medication, and has no medical or psychiatric history that may complicate the process, then withdrawal at home may be appropriate (Hayashida et al., 1989). Even in cases of severe and medicated withdrawal, medication may be administered at home where conditions permit (Stockwell, Bolt, Milner, Pugh, & Young, 1990).

Where inpatient detoxification is warranted – that is, where the severity of dependence (and thus complications) are likely to be high, or where there are no supportive relatives or friends to assist with home monitoring – purpose-built detoxification units rather than acute medical wards provide the best conditions for inpatient withdrawal (Alterman, Hayashida, & O'Brien, 1988; Pedersen, 1986).

Detoxification is often confused with treatment. Mattick and Hall (1996) point out that, although detoxification is an important component of treatment for those addicted and is a first step, especially where the degree of dependence is great, it is not appropriate to consider detoxification as a treatment in its own right because people who have undergone detoxification programmes are equally as likely to relapse as those who have not. Matthick and Hall note that the benefits of detoxification in general arise because of (1) the opportunity it provides for a change in lifestyle with the help of other interventions and (2) harm reduction effects where continued heavy alcohol usage could lead to serious complications, including death.

Alcoholics Anonymous

Alcoholics Anonymous (AA) is the oldest and the most well-known and utilized treatment intervention for alcohol dependence. Despite its longevity and public profile there is little research on its efficacy. This arises in part from one of the tenets of the organization, which holds that all members shall remain anonymous, and research or collection of any personal details is discouraged. Tonigan, Toscova, and Miller (1996), in a review that was intended to determine the variables that moderate research findings, located a broad variety of studies, which incorporated AA as a component of treatment. However, the quality of research of the 74 studies they located was not of sufficient standard to draw any conclusions on the effectiveness of AA. Mattick and Jarvis (1993) concluded that AA provides an accessible avenue for self-help and ongoing social support for those who choose abstinence as their goal, but there is no convincing evidence that AA alone is effective. Since then Project MATCH (see below) has provided some evidence that a treatment programme aimed to introduce alcohol-dependent patients to the teachings of AA (twelve-step facilitation therapy) produced equivalent drinking outcomes at 12 months to cognitive behavioural therapy and motivational enhancement treatment (Project MATCH Research Group, 1997).

Pharmacotherapies

There are a limited number of drugs that can be used to assist people with alcohol problems to become and remain abstinent. One of the first pharmacotherapies was disulfiram, marketed as Antabuse. This medicine is classed as an "antidipsotropic". It inhibits the enzyme that catalyses the breakdown of acetaldehyde in the blood. Ingestion of alcohol raises the acetaldehyde levels that causes nausea, vomiting, and shortness of breath. It has proved useful for problem drinkers who are highly motivated towards abstinence but has had limited success because of low rates of compliance, with many drinkers either discontinuing their medication, or deliberately missing doses in order to drink.

Schuckit (1996), in his review of recent developments in this area, concluded that evidence for the clinical effectiveness of disulfiram is modest at best; and that the use of this treatment needs to be carefully considered in view of the risks of side-effects such as peripheral neuropathy and hepatitis.

Newer antidipsotropics have included citrated calcium carbonate, which causes severe illness in patients who consume alcohol via a different mechanism to disulfiram. Similar problems with compliance have been observed. Some recent commentators (e.g., Heather, 1992) have suggested that antidipsotropics have an important place in the treatment of clients who are well motivated and have supplementary psychotherapy or counselling for their problem.

More recently an improved understanding of brain neurobiology has led to new pharmacological treatments to assist in relapse prevention. Approximately 50% of people who are alcohol dependent relapse within 3 months of treatment. The efficacy of the new drugs acamprosate and naltrexone in preventing relapse in people with alcohol dependence has been demonstrated in randomized controlled trials (Volpicelli, 1992; Whitworth et al., 1996). As with disulfiram, a limitation on efficacy is patient compliance. Naltrexone is superior to placebo only in compliant subjects.

Cognitive behavioural therapy

Cognitive behavioural therapy (CBT) aims to teach individuals how to control their responses to their environment through improving social, coping, and problem-solving skills. It is widely agreed by experts in the field that CBT is an important and effective treatment for abuse of alcohol (Hester, 1995). It appears to be most effective for individuals who have less severe alcohol-related problems and have had a shorter duration of drinking problems (Hester & Delaney, 1997).

Sitharthan, Kavanagh, and Sayer (1996) evaluated the effectiveness of CBT by correspondence for the treatment of individuals who were not alcoholics but felt they were drinking too much and wanted to reduce their alcohol intake. Two variations of CBT were included in the evaluation; one involving full treatment and the other involving minimal intervention. Both treatment programmes ran for a 4-month period during which subjects received 5 letters. Subjects in the minimal intervention condition received letters containing information about the effects of alcohol; they were encouraged to monitor their alcohol intake and send the monitoring cards to the researchers.

Each week these subjects were also asked to evaluate their alcohol intake. Subjects in the full treatment condition also received 5 letters that began with the same information. In addition, these subjects were given information on strategies to reduce their drinking. Suggested strategies included dealing with urges and temptations, problem-solving and planning for high-risk situations, goal-setting for alcohol intake, recording situations where goals were exceeded, relapse prevention, and planning of future lifestyle. Further, these subjects received follow-up letters encouraging continued use of these strategies and suggesting re-engagement after a lapse.

Subjects in both the full treatment and the minimal intervention groups showed significant improvements in self-efficacy and drinking behaviour post-treatment, and there was some evidence of a greater decline in alcohol consumption for the full treatment group. Again, the lack of an untreated control group means that the effectiveness of either CBT programme was not directly assessed.

Hester and Delaney (1997) completed a controlled study of the effectiveness of CBT for controlled drinking, using a computer programme to teach behavioural self-control. The study included 40 volunteers who scored at least 8 on the AUDIT (Saunders et al., 1993) but who scored below 20 on the MAST (Selzer, 1971). Those who scored 20 or more were considered more suitable for a programme with an abstinence goal. In order to be included in the outcome analysis, subjects had to complete at least 3 of the 8 therapy programme sessions that were administered over 10 weeks. Twenty subjects were randomly assigned to immediate treatment and 20 to 10 weeks delayed treatment. Follow-ups were scheduled at 10 weeks, 20 weeks, and 12 months. There were no significant pre-treatment differences between the two groups. At the 10-week mark, the immediately treated group showed significant improvement in drinking outcomes on baseline, and compared with the (then untreated) delayed group. The delayed group then received the CBT and improved significantly over the next 10 weeks at which time the two groups no longer differed. As gains were maintained at 12 months for the whole sample, this study supports CBT as an effective therapy.

One important area where CBT has been found to have potential to indirectly influence alcohol intake is in the treatment of alcoholics with comorbid depression. Brown, Evans, Miller, Burgess, and Mueller (1997) quote prior research evidence that suggests as many as 65–85% of patients entering alcohol treatment have clinically significant levels of depressive symptoms. Depression has been associated with poorer outcomes from alcohol treatment probably because depressed mood can trigger alcohol relapse. As CBT has been shown to be effective in treating unipolar depression, it is perhaps not surprising that CBT for depression also improved the achievement and maintenance of alcohol treatment goals.

CBT is an effective treatment procedure that appears to work best with non-dependent problem drinkers. One important CBT approach has been social skills training, which has some of the strongest evidence of outcome efficacy (Monti, Rosenow, Colby, & Abrams, 1995) This intervention assists the client to learn effective coping skills to manage problems with personal (thoughts, emotions) and social (interpersonal communication, stress, conflict) situations. For many problem drinkers, alcohol is the preferred means of coping with many difficult or threatening situations. Thus, training in social skills should help problem drinkers to overcome many of the major triggers for relapse. The evidence for this approach has been consistently strong (Miller et al., 1995), and it has also proved to be a popular form of intervention with both therapists and clients. This style of intervention, like all CBT approaches, has the advantage of being deliverable in either group or individual format.

Project MATCH (1997) was one of the largest treatment outcome studies in alcohol research. It examined the matching hypothesis that individuals will have a better outcome if they are matched to treatment on the basis of a set of characteristics. It involved matching alcohol-dependent clients to three different treatments with reference to a variety of client attributes. Two parallel randomized clinical trials were undertaken. One trial used clients enrolled for outpatient therapy ($N = 952$), while the other involved clients who had undergone residential treatment for at least 1 month prior to the study and were classified as being in aftercare ($N = 774$). Treatment strategies, client-matching variables, and the specific hypotheses for the study were based on theoretical considerations and prior empirical findings.

Three treatment strategies were compared. CBT was based on social learning theory that assumes alcohol abuse stems from negative life experiences, and thus the treatment addressed skills deficits and coping with situations where relapse was likely to occur. Twelve-step facilitation therapy (TSF) was based on the concept of alcoholism as a spiritual and medical disease and aimed to foster participation in the fellowship activities of AA. Motivational enhancement therapy (MET) focused on motivational strategies that are aimed at mobilizing the individual's own resources rather than specifying a particular path to recovery. There are several strategies that can be incorporated into a motivational enhancement therapy, one of which is exploring the pros and cons of continuing alcohol misuse. This strategy is designed to help the individual to express concern about alcohol use. The individual is prompted to consider the situation by listing the "good things" (PROS) and "less good things" (CONS) about alcohol use.

Sue, 26 years old, was in treatment for problems with alcohol. She was drinking more than 10 standard drinks a day. She filled out the following list early in her treatment:

PROS and CONS ratings for Sue

PROS	CONS
1. Relaxation	1. Cost of drinks
2. Drinking with friends	2. Hangovers and headaches
3. Helps me forget things	3. Guilt

Another key strategy is to help the client to think about his or her past life and compare this with how things seem at the present time. The life satisfaction strategy uses the discrepancy between how things are and how they were, or could be. The individual is asked "When you were (age) what did you think you would be doing now?" It is then possible to explore discrepancies between past expectations and the current situation. The aim is to guide links between drug and alcohol use and goals and aspirations.

Irrespective of treatment strategy, there were substantial positive changes in percent days abstinent and average number of drinks per drinking day in both aftercare and outpatient subjects at the 12-month follow-up. For example, prior to treatment, aftercare patients were abstinent approximately 20% of days per month, while at post-treatment and at 15 months they were abstinent for 90% of days in the last month. The equivalent figures for the outpatients were 23% pre- and 80% post-treatment days abstinent in the past month.

There were no consistent and clinically meaningful differences between the three treatments in outcome at 12 months in either the aftercare or outpatient groups. The study also found little support for the matching hypothesis. Only one attribute showed a significant interaction with treatment type: the outpatient group with low psychiatric severity showed more abstinent days in the 12-step treatment than they did in the CBT approach.

As the authors note, the general lack of support for the matching hypothesis from this study does not mean that matching is never of value. The sample specifically excluded subjects with multiple forms of drug dependence and the homeless who would be regarded as being at greater than average risk on a variety of measures. It is also possible that treatments for illicit drug abuse may fit the matching hypothesis and that matching may work with pharmacological treatments.

Family and marital therapy

The purpose of family and marital therapy is to engage significant others in the rehabilitation of individuals who abuse alcohol. Various types of family therapy have been trialled: systems, interactional, behavioural, and spouse-directed (Mattick & Jarvis, 1993). The contingency-based community reinforcement approach (CRA), developed by Azrin et al. (1996), also aims to engage those close to the affected person in a behaviorally oriented approach to treatment. CRA was developed as a more intensive and broad-ranging approach that addresses community reinforcers both within and outside the family in an effort to encourage interests and activities, which lead to abstinence. CRA tends to involve close family members and is thus incorporated with behavioural family and marital approaches for the purposes of this review.

In a comprehensive review of the alcohol treatment outcome literature, Mattick and Jarvis (1993) found that behavioural marital therapy (BMT) was more effective than no treatment at all, but was no more effective than individual alcohol counselling or brief advice and follow-up. In their analysis of CRA, they found good support for its use in the short term, but concluded that more research was required to ascertain long-term effects as well as the specific effects of supervised disulfiram on CRA outcomes.

A recent study by Smith, Meyers, and Delaney (1998) considered the relative advantages of the CRA approach compared with standard treatment (STD) given at a large day shelter for homeless alcohol-dependent individuals. They found that both groups improved significantly following treatment and that those engaged in CRA treatment had significantly superior outcomes to the STD group. However, there were problems in the design of the study in that, in order to retain the significant benefits of being on the programmes (including housing), those engaged in CRA were required to show greater discipline in participation than the STD group. There were also greater checks and punishments for the CRA group for lapses in drinking while participating. Thus, as the authors point out, the study did not adequately compare the two specified treatments, and therefore does not provide conclusive evidence of the superiority of the CRA approach compared with usual care.

Evidence for the efficacy of the CRA approach is based on a very small number of controlled outcome studies. As summarized by Baucom, Mueser, Daiuto, and Stickle (1998), most recent research on BMT includes the use of partner-assistance in maintaining disulfiram contracts as well as motivational pre-sessions as part of the therapy that may confound the effects of the behavioural therapy alone. Similarly, CRA can be considered as a bundle of treatments of varying effectiveness. More evidence on the total package as well as the components, and more replication by other research groups is required, before the effectiveness of BMT alone, or CRA, can be clarified.

Given the lack of good clinical trials with sufficient power, which directly assess the effectiveness of BMT, there is little evidence that inclusion of the spouse or significant others in treatment is any more effective than individual treatment.

Summary

Assessment is an important first step in the treatment of alcohol problems. There are a range of standardized measures of alcohol dependence and screening instruments, such as AUDIT, that can be used to determine the severity of a client's alcohol-related problems. Given the high prevalence of depression among heavy drinkers, assessment of the severity of dependence may be useful.

One-to-one intensive interventions are not required for everyone who has a problem with alcohol use. Public health interventions to advise drinkers of safe levels of drinking have a role to play. So too does screening for hazardous alcohol use in primary health care and other settings where adults who drink hazardously and harmfully are to be found. Persons who are drinking hazardously can be given simple advice on how to reduce or moderate their alcohol consumption. Moderation rather than abstinence is an appropriate therapeutic goal for patients with mild to moderate levels of alcohol dependence.

Patients with more severe forms of dependence should be encouraged to become abstinent.

A range of treatment approaches are available for patients or clients whose alcohol problems have resisted self-help efforts to moderate or quit. One of the oldest is the self-help fellowship of AA, which is of assistance in helping some alcohol-dependent people to remain abstinent but is not attractive to all patients. Pharmacotherapies such as disulfiram, naltrexone, and acomprosate may assist some patients to remain abstinent and avert relapse to drinking. Ensuring adequate compliance with the drugs is a major issue.

A number of psychological interventions are of value in the treatment of alcohol dependence, including cognitive behavioural therapy (CBT), motivational enhancement therapy (MET), twelve-step facilitation therapy (TSF), and family and marital therapy (FMT). In studies to date these treatments seem to be of equivalent efficacy in unselected patients and there does not appear to be any particular value in attempting to match patients to treatment on any basis other than patient choice.

Nicotine 6

Introduction

Tobacco is one of the most widely used psychoactive substances in the general population. It has an extremely high dependence liability – higher than the opiates, alcohol, and other controlled substances (Anthony et al., 1994).

Over the past five decades evidence has accumulated on the adverse effects of tobacco-smoking on health (Novello, 1990; US Department of Health, Education and Welfare, 1964, 1971, 1979, 1984, 1988). Exposure to tobacco smoke has also been identified as a cause of 32 different diseases (Environmental Protection Agency, 1992; Royal College of Physicians of London, 1992; US Surgeon General, 1982, 1986), as well as being a cause of fire injuries.

Smoking is the single most preventable cause of death globally (Center for Disease Control and Prevention, 1992). The World Health Organization has identified tobacco-smoking as one of the major causes of burden of illness (Murray & Lopez, 1996). In 1992 smoking in Australia accounted for more than two-thirds (67%) of the total social cost of drug abuse (Collins & Lapsley, 1996) and in 1997 was estimated to have caused around 18,000 deaths (Williams, 1998).

Given the burden of disease caused by smoking and the low cost of smoking cessation treatments, these interventions are among the most cost-effective in medicine when measured in terms of the cost of increasing quality-adjusted life years (Murray & Lopez, 1996).

Assessment

Assessment should include three aspects: motivation to quit, smoking history, and nicotine dependence. Assessment of motivation to quit smoking may be done simply by assessing readiness to change (Laforge, Velicer, Richmond, & Owen, 1999). This may be done by asking "Are you seriously considering quitting smoking?". Smokers may be categorized as precontemplative, contemplative, or in a preparation stage. The response of the client to the above question may indicate a need for motivational interviewing, particularly if the person seems to be ambivalent about his or her smoking (Mattick & Baillie, 1992).

A range of factors related to smoking need to be considered in assessment (Henningfield, Lakshmi, & Shiffman, 1998). The first of these is the client's smoking history and level of nicotine dependence. Research suggests that persons who are more severely dependent on nicotine may have greater difficulty in remaining abstinent, and so may require a more intensive intervention (e.g., the use of nicotine replacement therapy, antidepressant).

Perhaps the most widely used measure of nicotine dependence in clinical settings is the Fagerström Test for Nicotine Dependence (see Table 6.1; Heatherton, Kozlowski, Frecker, & Fagerström, 1991). This is a measure of nicotine dependence with a score ranging from 0 to 10, with higher scores indicating higher levels of dependence.

Questions about the smoking history of clients may also be useful. This could include the number of years they have regularly smoked, and previous quit attempts (and what interventions, if any, were used to assist them). This knowledge can help to formulate an appropriate intervention plan, but persons who have smoked for many years, from a young age, and who have previously attempted to quit smoking, may require more intensive assistance to stop smoking.

Monitoring of withdrawal symptoms is an important component of the smoking cessation intervention (Mattick & Baillie, 1992). As withdrawal symptoms are predictive of relapse to smoking, careful attention to this possibility needs to be paid in the planning of the quit attempt. Symptoms of nicotine withdrawal include craving for a cigarette, depressed mood, difficulty falling asleep, awakening at night, irritability, frustration or anger, anxiety, difficulty concentrating, restlessness, and increased appetite.

One measure that might be used is the Shiffman Tobacco Withdrawal Scale, which shows changes in scores as a function of time since the last cigarette smoked and differentiates between partial and total abstinence (Shiffman & Jarvik, 1976). The severity of each symptom can be scored by the subject on a 5-point scale as: absent, slight, mild, moderate, or severe.

TABLE 6.1

The revised Fagerström test for nicotine dependence

a. How soon after waking do you smoke your first cigarette?
    3   Within 5 minutes
    2   6–30 minutes
    1   31–60 minutes

b. Do you find it difficult to abstain from smoking in places where it is forbidden? E.g. church, library, etc.
    1   Yes
    0   No

c. Which cigarette would you hate to give up?
    1   The first one in the morning
    0   Any other

d. How many cigarettes a day do you smoke?
    0   10 or less
    1   11 to 20
    2   21 to 30
    3   31 or more

e. Do you smoke more frequently in the morning than in the rest of the day?
    1   Yes
    0   No

f. Do you smoke even though you are sick in bed for most of the day?
    1   Yes
    0   No

Score:
0–2 = very low dependence;   3–4 = low dependence;   5 = medium dependence;   6–7 = high dependence;   8+ = very high dependence.

Depression decreases the likelihood that attempts to quit smoking will be successful (Anda et al., 1990), and depressed mood is a common symptom of nicotine withdrawal (Madden et al., 1997). Furthermore, there is some association between anxiety disorders and smoking. It has been suggested, similarly to depression, that persons with anxiety may also find it more difficult to stop smoking (Gilbert & Gilbert, 1995).

Interventions

A variety of approaches to smoking cessation have been developed (Agency for Health Care Policy and Research, 1996; Fiore, Bailey, &

Cohen, 1996) from nicotine replacement therapy to cognitive behavioural interventions. The Agency for Health Care Policy and Research Smoking Cessation Clinical Practice Guideline Staff have outlined the general principles of therapy. One of the first steps is formulating a quit plan.

If a person is willing to make a quit attempt, then assistance can be given in the formulation of a quit plan (Agency for Health Care Policy and Research, 1996). This may consist of the following elements:

1. Setting a date for quitting tobacco use. This date should ideally be within one or two weeks.
2. Assisting the client with his or her preparation for the quit attempt. This may include a number of elements, including:
   (a) the client telling others that a quitting attempt is being made and asking for their support;
   (b) removing cigarettes from the client's environment;
   (c) going over previous attempts to quit (if any) and examining what elements were helpful or not so helpful to the client; and
   (d) examining anything that may be a challenge to the success of the quit attempt, particularly in the early stages.

Given the difficulties associated with achieving and maintaining abstinence from smoking, there are a number of ways in which the client may be informed of pitfalls to success and suggestions for minimizing the likelihood that he or she will return to smoking (Agency for Health Care Policy and Research, 1996). This may be achieved using a brief intervention in which the client is informed of some of the issues to consider regarding the quit attempt, and some of the things that can be done to make success more likely.

A meta-analysis of individual counselling of clients for smoking cessation was conducted by the Cochrane collaboration group (Lancaster & Stead, 2000). Individual counselling was defined as a face-to-face meeting between a client and a trained smoking cessation counsellor (counselling by doctors or nurses as part of clinical care was excluded). Sessions all involved more than 10 minutes of contact, and typically included: a review of smoking history, motivation to quit, identification of high-risk situations, and related problem-solving strategies. Some also included the provision of written material. Control groups were given usual care and up to 10 minutes of advice.

The analysis found that individual counselling significantly improved the chances of successful smoking cessation compared to controls. The researchers concluded that "smoking cessation counselling can assist smokers to quit" (Lancaster & Stead, 2000). Interestingly, there was no difference between intensive and briefer counselling programmes, suggesting that a brief intervention may be just as effective as a more intensive one, although the authors of the study cautioned that they could not exclude the possibility that a more intensive intervention may have been more helpful in assisting quit attempts (Lancaster & Stead, 2000).

A meta-analysis of group counselling for smoking cessation found that group programmes were more effective than no intervention or minimal contact interventions (Stead & Lancaster, 2000). There was no evidence that manipulating the social interactions between participants in a group programme had an effect on outcome. No difference in cessation rates was found in a comparison of individual and group counselling interventions (Lancaster & Stead, 2000). There was limited evidence that adding group counselling to other forms of treatment, including advice from a health professional or nicotine replacement, increased the effectiveness of cessation attempts. The authors concluded that "there is evidence that groups are better than self-help, and other less intensive interventions. There is not enough evidence on their effectiveness compared to intensive individual counselling" (Stead & Lancaster, 2000).

Among the more important issues to consider are:

1. Make abstinence the goal of the quit attempt, as research suggests that any smoking increases the chances that a full relapse to smoking will occur (Mattick & Baillie, 1992).
2. Inform the patient about the nature of withdrawal symptoms and the length of time for which they are likely to continue. Withdrawal symptoms may include cravings, depressed mood, sleeping problems, irritability, and increased appetite. Withdrawal symptoms typically begin a few hours after cessation of smoking, and peak 24 to 72 hours (Mattick & Baillie, 1992). They may continue in a less intense fashion for between a week and a month;
3. Be aware of the triggers for relapse. These include drinking alcohol, and sharing a household with smokers. The client might consider avoiding drinking alcohol for a short period; and perhaps coordinate the quit attempt with other smokers, or make plans to maintain abstinence in the household.

Nicotine replacement therapy

The development of nicotine replacement therapy (NRT) has been a major advance in smoking cessation. Smokers who have a medium to high score ($\geq$5) on the Fagerström Test for Nicotine Dependence (Heatherton et al., 1991) are likely to be addicted to nicotine and are therefore good candidates for NRT. Such smokers may experience withdrawal symptoms during the first two weeks of not smoking. NRT is designed to reduce craving for a cigarette and helps to prevent withdrawal symptoms (Pomerleau & Pomerleau, 1988).

The forms of NRT include nicotine patches, nicotine gum, nasal sprays, and inhalers. These have different speeds of onset, peak plasma levels of nicotine, and duration of effects, with the slowest acting being nicotine patches, and the most immediate being nasal sprays (Stitzer & DeWit, 1998). Nasal sprays and inhalers were more effective than nicotine patches or gum; however, nicotine patches are the most studied form among the NRT products. A summary of the research is given below.

Transdermal nicotine patch

One of the most popular forms of NRT is the transdermal patch, which works by delivering a fairly steady plasma concentration of nicotine. It is designed to provide constant protection from withdrawal symptoms and craving for cigarettes while the patient focuses on changing the behavioural aspects of the smoking habit (Benowitz, 1998; Fiore, Smith, Jorenby, & Baker, 1994; Mendelson & Richmond, 1994).

Meta-analyses of the transdermal nicotine patch have found that the quit rates of those who receive an active patch are typically more than double those who used placebo patches (Fiore et al., 1996; Silagy, Mant, Fowler, & Lodge, 1994). Studies of the effectiveness of these products suggest that replacement therapies increase the odds of successful cessation by 70%, with rates of 19% abstinent at 1 year compared to 11% of controls (Silagy et al., 1994). One Australian study recently found that, at 12 months, an active patch produced 28% quit rates, compared to 12% for placebo (Richmond, Kehoe, & Neto, 1997).

Correct use of the patch is safe and generally well tolerated (Richmond et al., 1997). Some may experience side-effects including transient itching, burning and tingling, contact dermatitis, contact urticaria, disturbed sleep, and abnormal dreams (with the 24-hour patch) (Gourlay, 1994). It has now been shown that nicotine patches do not have clinically significant adverse cardiovascular effects, even in people with heart disease who use nicotine patches while continuing to smoke (Benowitz & Gourlay, 1997). Also, the risk of developing dependence has been found to be minimal with nicotine patches (Henningfield & Keenan, 1993).

Antidepressant drugs

Recent advances in research surrounding smoking cessation have revealed that antidepressant drugs may be particularly effective in assisting persons to stop smoking. A broad range of antidepressant drugs has been trialled as aids to nicotine withdrawal and are of particular relevance for those with a history of prior episodes of depression, or for those who have a history of failed quit attempts, and may require a more intensive intervention to help them to quit successfully.

Two antidepressant drugs, bupropion and nortriptyline, have been found to be among the most effective (Hughes, Stead, & Lancaster, 1999) and post little or no risk of dependence. Bupropion has effects on dopaminergic and noradrenergic transmission, and has been approved by the USA for use as a smoking cessation aid (Hughes et al., 1999). Nortriptyline is a tricyclic antidepressant with adrenergic activity.

Bupropion

The studies conducted to date suggest that bupropion significantly improves cessation attempts compared to placebo (Hurt et al., 1997; Jorenby et al., 1999). One clinical study found that, at 1 year, cessation rates for those given bupropion were almost double those given placebo (23 : 12%; both were given behavioural therapy) (Hurt et al., 1997). A recent randomized controlled trial using sustained release bupropion reported that bupropion more than doubled smoking cessation rates over placebo (Jorenby et al., 1999). This finding was observed irrespective of whether smokers were given NRT.

The most common adverse reactions to bupropion are insomnia and dry mouth (Hebert, 1999; Hurt et al., 1997). Other less common reactions include pruritus, urticaria, oedema, tremors, and dizziness (Hebert, 1999). There appears to be a small risk of convulsions (estimated at 1 case per 1,000; McAfee & France, 1998). However, one study found that when volunteers were screened, no seizures were observed in any of the 2,400 subjects (Hurt et al., 1997). There have been some case reports of cardiovascular reactions following the use of bupropion (Hebert, 1999), but in a recent discussion of the use of this drug, it was suggested that screening for vulnerability to seizures or heart problems would minimize these risks (Hughes et al., 1999).

Research has suggested that the combined use of nicotine patches and bupropion does not significantly increase cessation rates compared to bupropion alone (Jorenby et al., 1999).

Nortriptyline

Research into the use of nortriptyline has found that it significantly aided smokers in their quit attempt (Hall et al., 1998a; Hughes et al., 1999). Persons given nortriptyline were over twice as likely to achieve continuous abstinence than those given a placebo (abstinence rates of 24% and 12%, respectively, at 64 weeks).

This study also examined quit rates among those with and without a history of major depression and found that persons with a history of major depression were no more likely than those without such a history to achieve abstinence when given the treatment (Hall et al., 1998a). However, they were also no *less* likely to quit; and given the fact that persons with depression have been estimated to be 40% less likely to quit than non-depressed smokers (Anda et al., 1990), nortriptyline may have served to increase the quitting rate among those with a history of depression to a level similar to persons without depression.

Other therapies

As with many chronic or relapsing conditions, a large number of approaches have been advocated to assist smokers to quit successfully, but have little or no supportive evidence of their effectiveness. These are briefly listed below:

1. *Acupuncture.* A Cochrane review of the evidence concerning acupuncture as an aid to quit smoking compared it with (a) sham acupuncture, (b) other interventions, and (c) no intervention (White, Rampes, & Ernst, 2000). They found that 18 studies has been published, and 20 comparisons made. Acupuncture was not superior to sham acupuncture, other interventions, or control interventions. The authors concluded that "there is no clear evidence that acupuncture is effective for smoking cessation" (White et al., 2000).
2. *Aversive smoking.* Aversion therapy pairs the pleasurable stimulus of smoking a cigarette with some unpleasant stimulus, thus

extinguishing the urge to smoke. A study of the efficacy of aversive smoking in randomized trials that compared aversion treatments with "inactive" procedures (Hajek & Stead, 2000) found that the odds of abstinence following aversive smoking was doubled compared to that of a control. The authors concluded that because of the lack of biochemical validation of abstinence, "this finding should be interpreted cautiously" (Hajek & Stead, 2000). Other aversion methods were not shown to be effective and Hajek and Stead recommended further research into the efficacy of aversive smoking with more rigorous methodology.

3. *Hypnotherapy.* Hypnotherapy has been promoted as a method for aiding smoking cessation by acting on underlying impulses, and (a) weakening the desire to smoke or (b) strengthening the will to stop. A review of the research on hypnotherapy found that "the effects of hypnotherapy on smoking cessation claimed by uncontrolled studies were not confirmed by analysis of randomized controlled trials" (Abbot, Stead, White, Barnes, & Ernst, 2000).

Summary

Because of the burden of disease that tobacco-smoking causes, interventions to assist smokers to stop are among the most cost-effective in medicine.

Assessment of smokers need not be elaborate. The major question of the smoker's nicotine dependence can be assessed by the Fagerström scale. Its relevance is in deciding whether the smoker may be helped to deal with withdrawal symptoms by nicotine replacement treatment. Effective interventions involve:

- motivating smokers to quit
- formulating a quit plan, including a quit date
- providing counselling
- nicotine replacement for nicotine dependence
- antidepressants such as buproprion and nortryptaline particularly for smokers in whom depressive symptoms may lead to relapse to smoking.

Interventions for which there is either no evidence or weak evidence of efficacy include: acupuncture, aversive smoking, and hypnotherapy.

Cannabis 7

Introduction

The drug *cannabis* is the most widely abused illicit drug in the developed world. Cannabis is the generic name given to the collection of materials derived from different parts of the *Cannabis sativa* plant, chiefly the flowering buds and leaves from the upper parts of the mature plant. The buds or "heads" are rich in a sticky, resinous substance that contains high concentrations of cannabinoid compounds. Although numerous cannabinoids have been identified in the cannabis plant, the primary psychoactive constituent is a single cannabinoid named delta-9-tetrahydrocannabinol (Δ^9-THC). THC is to cannabis as nicotine is to tobacco: different plants and plant strains of varying quality may yield differing quantities of THC, and the means of both preparation and administration of the cannabis plant material influences the amount of THC available to the consumer. Ultimately, in producing the primary psychoactive effects of cannabis consumption, THC, like nicotine, is the substance primarily responsible for the psychoactive effects sought by users.

A number of other terms are applied to cannabis products, the most common of which is marijuana; other popular names include dope, mull, pot, weed, and grass. Forms of cannabis grown hydroponically (i.e., in an enriched substrate without soil) are known as "hydro", and one popular hybrid form is known as "skunk".

Cannabis is predominantly administered by smoking, and so the form of cannabis used is prepared with the aim of maximizing the amount of THC available in the smoke of the burnt plant matter. This is usually achieved by smoking the dried resinous buds and upper leaves of the plant. Cannabis "heads" are favoured for their potency; however, some users smoke the bulky cannabis leaf, which has low

THC levels and usually delivers a harsh, acrid smoke owing to the high levels of tar and other substances present in the burnt plant material.

Alternative forms that deliver greater concentrations of THC include hashish (or "hash"), which is a crude extraction of cannabis resin, compressed in blocks for consumption by smoking. A relatively unusual form of cannabis is the highly purified oil extracted from hashish, which may contain as much as 20% THC. This is also smoked, after a small amount is added to a tobacco cigarette or pipe.

All forms of cannabis product, including leaf, heads, hashish, and hash oil, can be consumed with the greatest degree of pharmacological efficiency by smoking. Perhaps the best-known form of cannabis-smoking is via the "joint" or hand-rolled cannabis cigarette, which may be prepared with or without a quantity of tobacco. However, an increasingly popular method of administration, because of its efficiency in delivering THC with little waste of sidestream smoke, is the water pipe, or "bong". The bong is usually made of a small bottle or jar half filled with water, which allows the cannabis smoke to be cooled as it is drawn from the "cone" through the water-filled chamber in a single, large inhalation. Heads, leaf, and hash may all be consumed via a joint or a bong. Recent research has shown that while bongs maximize the amount of THC consumed, they also increase the amount of tar and other harmful materials consumed per dose, compared with joints (Gowing, Ali, & White, 2000).

It is important to note that THC can also be delivered effectively via other routes. These usually involve preparing cannabis heads or hash in small cakes or cookies and eating them, or suffusing cannabis material in hot water and drinking the resulting brew. While these methods provide satisfactory psychoactive effects, they are not popular with most cannabis users because the time to onset of the effect is much slower than smoking, and the dose is more difficult to judge.

Assessment

Like most other psychoactive substances, which produce euphoric effects, the regular, heavy use of cannabis may result in a cannabis-dependence syndrome. While the existence of cannabis dependence has been a contentious issue for some years, there is now a growing body of evidence that suggests there is a cannabis-dependence syndrome that is consistent with that of other classic drugs of dependence.

Regular use of cannabis produces a marked tolerance, similar to other drugs of abuse and dependence, and there is now evidence that cannabis also produces a withdrawal syndrome (Hall et al., 1994). The general descriptive criteria developed by Edwards et al. (1981) to apply to all drug dependencies has been applied to cannabis (Swift, Copeland, & Hall, 1997) in the most recent editions of the *International Classification of Mental and Behavioural Disorders* (World Health Organization, 1993) and the *Diagnostic and Statistical Manual of Mental Disorders* (American Psychiatric Association, 1994). These nosologies allow the operationalization of the dependence syndrome by defining several basic criteria that reflect the salience that the user has come to place on the use of the drug, above other behaviours (Teesson, Lynskey, Manor, & Baillie, submitted).

Research on long-term cannabis users in Australia has confirmed the appropriateness of the DSM-IV criteria for diagnosing cannabis dependence. In a study of 268 long-term, heavy cannabis users from the North Coast area of New South Wales, just over half of the sample met DSM-III-R criteria for cannabis dependence. The most common symptoms included: frequent intoxication or use during daily activities, tolerance, and continued use despite problems (Didcott, Reilly, Swift, & Hall, 1997). The quantity of cannabis typically used by the study participants was correlated with their degree of cannabis dependence. This sample comprised males and females in their late thirties to early forties, who had been using cannabis on average for 19 years. The sample had a higher rate of respiratory problems and accidental injury than the general population.

A further study by Swift et al. (1997) of 200 long-term cannabis users from Sydney confirmed the existence of a cannabis-dependence syndrome among this population. Participants in this study comprised males and females, aged in their late twenties, who had been using cannabis for an average of 11 years. Over half of the sample used cannabis daily, and three-quarters used cannabis on at least 4 days per week. Most of the sample used heads, and administered these with a bong, thus maximizing the amount of THC delivered per usage. Almost half of the sample had experienced problems with other drugs, and one-quarter had a history of problem drinking. The prevalence of cannabis dependence in this sample was higher than their North Coast counterparts, with 92% meeting DSM-III-R criteria. Level of dependence was correlated with cannabis consumption level and psychological distress.

There is a small but consistent demand for professional help with cannabis-related problems in Australia, the USA, and Europe. The National Census of Clients of Australian Treatment Service Agencies (Torres, Mattick, Chen, & Baillie, 1995) found that the proportion of cases for which cannabis was the *main* drug problem increased from 4% in 1990 to 7% in 1995. Between 1994 and 1998 cannabis was the primary drug of abuse for between 11 and 26% of clients of treatment agencies in the USA (US Office of National Drug Control Policy, 1998) and was also the primary drug problem for between 2 and 16% of clients attending treatment agencies in the European Union in 1998 (European Monitoring Centre for Drugs and Drug Addiction, 1998).

Stephens, Roffman, and Simpson (1994a) recruited 382 people into a controlled trial of two types of cannabis-specific treatment over 3 months. Their clients reported the following adverse consequences of cannabis use in the 90 days before assessment: inability to stop using (93%), feeling bad about abusing cannabis (87%), procrastinating (86%), loss of self-confidence (76%), memory loss (67%), and withdrawal symptoms (51%). Symptoms related to the salience and compulsive nature of their cannabis use were most common, and similar data have been reported from recent US (Budney, Bickel, & Amass, 1998; Stephens et al., 1994a) and Australian treatment trials of interventions for cannabis use (Rees, Copeland, & Swift, 1998).

Assessment may comprise a structured, clinical interview, in which key data pertaining to demographics, drug use, family history, pattern and history of cannabis use, past treatment experiences, and criminal history are obtained. In addition, clients may complete a number of self-administered instruments.

In addition, it may be useful to obtain a measure of the client's self-efficacy, or situational confidence to resist cannabis use in a range of situations. One such measure is the Cannabis Situational Confidence Questionnaire (Rees et al., 1998). The SCQ-39 (Annis & Graham, 1988) also measures self-efficacy, although is not cannabis-specific. Such a measure can be used to monitor clinically relevant changes over time, as well as provide important information about the client's profile of cannabis use at the time of assessment.

For diagnosis of cannabis dependence, DSM-IV criteria should be used to obtain a thorough appraisal of the client's cannabis-dependence symptoms. In addition, the Severity of Dependence Scale (SDS; Gossop et al., 1995) has been adapted from its primary purpose of assessment of heroin dependence to cannabis dependence (Swift et al., 1997). This scale provides an assessment of psychological aspects of cannabis dependence. Of these measures of dependence, the SDS is the briefest and most clinically useful instrument (Swift, Copeland, & Hall, 1998).

Interventions

Psychological interventions

There has been very little systematic development and evaluation of interventions for cannabis dependence. Most interventions used for cannabis dependence have been adaptations of alcohol interventions (Miller & Gold, 1998; Zweben & O'Connell, 1992). Because the central features of alcohol, tobacco, and cannabis dependence are similar, we can make tentative extrapolations from the alcohol treatment and cigarette-smoking cessation fields.

Controlled trials of cannabis interventions have used aversion therapy (Smith, Schmeling, & Knowles, 1988) and supportive expressive psychotherapy (Grenyer, Laborsky, & Solowij, 1995). As in the research from which these innovations were derived, little evidence was obtained for their efficacy in cannabis-dependence treatment.

Preliminary research has suggested that CBT interventions may have a role in the management of cannabis dependence – a finding that also reflects the state of research into nicotine- and alcohol-dependence treatment. Several randomized controlled trials of CBT for cannabis dependence have been performed recently in the USA by Roffman and Stephens and their colleagues. These studies have compared CBT with a basic skills training approach, both of which were tailored specifically to meet the unique demands of cannabis-dependent clients (Stephens, Roffman, & Simpson, 1994b). The interventions were delivered in a group format, and although there were no differences between the treatments in rates of abstinence 12 months after therapy, there were substantial reductions in the number of days of cannabis use and cannabis problems compared to pre-treatment. Overall, 20% of the sample were abstinent 1 year after the intervention, which is comparable to most studies of efficacy in alcohol (Mattick & Jarvis, 1993) and tobacco-smoking cessation (Mattick & Baillie, 1992). The CBT approach used by Roffman and Stephens clearly warrants further investigation.

A further development on the work of Roffman and colleagues has been undertaken in a large-scale randomized controlled trial of cannabis-dependence treatment, with promising outcomes (Rees et al., 1998). The basic structure of this intervention is described below.

Cognitive behavioural therapy for cannabis dependence

The CBT intervention outlined is based on an outpatient treatment format, with individual client therapy. The CBT programme is designed to be performed over a total of 6 structural therapy sessions, each of which lasts approximately 1 hour.

At a single assessment session, undertaken in the week prior to the commence of therapy, key data are obtained from the client and an outline of the nature and content of the therapy is given. Ideally, the timing and physical location of the therapy sessions should be as consistent as possible; that is, appointments for the same time and day should be made for each subsequent week, and the place should be held constant. This may help to optimize the establishment of a working rapport with the therapist and help the client to become comfortable with the therapeutic arrangements.

Delivery of a CBT intervention for cannabis dependence

This section outlines the content of the CBT programme used in the randomized controlled trial, and describes the procedure on a session-by-session basis.

Session 1

The main elements of this session involve setting the scene and introducing motivational enhancement training. Clients should be given the "ground-rules" of treatment, as well as an explanation of cognitive behavioural therapy. This may include a description of skills acquisition, especially drug-related skills (management of urges, dealing with high-risk situations), and general coping skills (cognitive restructuring, stress management, problem-solving skills).

It is usually useful to commence the intervention with feedback from assessment. Discuss the client's pattern of cannabis use, and consider the client's degree of dependence. Clients who score highly on the Severity of Dependence Scale (SDS) are often not surprised at their high level of dependence, but this fact can help to motivate them to make changes.

The main focus of the session should be on motivational enhance-ment training, and should cover issues such as setting goals, removing barriers to change, and identifying skills or techniques for enabling change. Behavioural self-monitoring is also a useful tool, to help the client to remain focused, or "on target", in achieving short-term goals.

Session 2

The focus is on helping the client to plan to quit. It reviews the week and homework exercises, and reviews personal triggers and high-risk situations. One of the most important skills required by clients in their first stages of quitting is coping with urges and cravings. It is also important that clients should understand how to deal with slips or lapses. This information is based on the relapse prevention training model of Marlatt and Gordon (1985).

A detailed plan for quitting should be developed with the client, with a quit date set for the following week. Information and discussion of withdrawal symptoms will also be important, if only to allay fears or concerns about possible discomforts. Clients should be encouraged to examine their social support systems, and make steps to recruit appropriate persons to lend general support.

Some clients will benefit from learning techniques to help them to refuse drugs, although drug refusal skills may not be necessary for all clients. Those who have relatively sophisticated communication skills will feel awkward being taught how to say no to a smoke.

The session should conclude with a discussion of the client's goals for the following week, and setting homework tasks.

Session 3

This session should assist the client to manage any withdrawal symptoms or problems that have arisen as a consequence of quitting in the last few days. For clients who have not quit, the problems or issues that are causing a hindrance should be addressed and resolved.

The session uses the technique of cognitive restructuring as the main focus. Its main aim is to assist the client to identify when he or she is thinking negatively or engaging in automatic patterns of thought that may lead to drug use. The techniques should assist the client to interrupt this (automatic) thinking. Finally, the client should learn to challenge negative thoughts and replace them with more positive ones that help to reduce the urge to use cannabis. One theme that appears common is the process of mental "justification" for smoking, despite having decided not to smoke.

The key concept of cognitive restructuring is that thinking influences the way a person feels and behaves. Introducing the client to practical strategies for changing negative thinking is a key aspect of overcoming much of the psychological aspects of cannabis dependence. An outline of cognitive restructuring techniques is provided in the text by Jarvis, Tebbit, and Mattick (1994).

Session 4

This session should continue the focus on cognitive strategies and begin training in further skills enhancement. After a review of the previous week's progress, determine how well the client has progressed in using thought-stopping or challenging techniques. Work with the client to overcome any problems that have arisen, and encourage the client to continue practising this skill, reminding him or her that it takes some persistence to change negative thinking.

The client should be given a choice of the personal skills to be developed in this session. These might include *problem-solving skills*, *management of insomnia*, or *progressive muscle relaxation* for managing stress.

Session 5

This second-last session should focus on reviewing and consolidating the skills introduced so far, and addressing any problems that have arisen. Clients should be introduced to new skills, if these are required and time permits. This is a decision that the therapist should make based on the client's needs and progress to date. Further skills might include coping skills training, which comprises techniques such as *assertiveness skills*, *communication skills*, and *stress or anger management*.

Session 6

The final session should concentrate on relapse prevention and lifestyle modification issues. The main ideas to be covered include the main elements of Marlatt and Gordon's (1985) relapse prevention training.

Relapse prevention is a crucial component of treatment in the addictions. The general aim of relapse prevention training is to provide the individual with skills to avoid lapses and prevent lapses from becoming relapses to alcohol and drug use. Relapse prevention aims to help clients to learn a range of skills to avoid lapses to harmful drug or alcohol use, and to acquire behavioural strategies and changes in thinking that lessen the negative impact of a slip turning into a full-blown lapse. Relapse prevention outlines relapses as opportunities to learn rather than indications of failure.

Relapse prevention has also developed the idea that behaviour change is usually not achieved successfully in isolation – that is, individuals who are successful usually make other adjustments to their lifestyle and move towards an overall healthier and more positive way of living that complement and reinforce the initial changes in drinking or drug use. Saunders and Allsop (1991) have promoted this approach as a way of improving outcomes of relapse prevention interventions.

The relapse prevention model

Successful relapse prevention and maintenance of initial change in use of alcohol or drugs is influenced to a large extent by the lifestyle of individuals. Therefore, relapse prevention training also involves examining lifestyle factors that can either hinder or support behaviour change. For example, a 25-year-old male who is single, cannabis dependent and uses heavily in social interactions may have a relapse prevention strategy quite different to a similar individual who is married. Relapse prevention training can be divided into the following areas:

- enhancing commitment to change
- identifying causes of relapse
- reintroducing useful strategies
- preparing for relapse
- identifying lifestyle issues important to maintaining initial change.

Enhancing commitment to change. Commitment to maintaining behavioural change is an essential component in relapse prevention training. The individual may benefit from reviewing the negative aspects of drug and alcohol use and the reasons for changing their patterns.

Identifying causes of relapse. Individuals may observe that relapse occurs following a clearly identifiable event or in particular situations – for example, when the individual is anxious or depressed, has experienced a relationship breakdown, or has been under considerable social pressure to drink or take drugs. Identifying high-risk situations involves attaining information: where, when, with whom, doing what, and feeling what?

A high-risk situation is one where an individual is highly vulnerable to relapse, and one where an individual has experienced a lapse or relapse in the past. Such situations are usually laden with cues or triggers for drug use or drinking, and these have the effect of promoting urges or cravings. Such thoughts or feelings are strongly bound with the temptation to drink or use a drug, and in the absence of some alternative coping technique the client is at high risk of relapse.

High-risk situations can be grouped into three main types. Situations that feature triggers of a negative emotional nature may involve internal triggers, such as depression, stress, anxiety, or even boredom. Because these states have, in the past, reliably preceded drug use, they may be closely linked with the urge to use. Clients without adequate coping skills in such situations are at risk of relapse. Another high-risk situation involves positive mood states, which also act as internal triggers that prime a positive incentive motivational state. These situations may include celebrations or social situations, and the use of alcohol or other drugs may serve to increase the pleasant feelings involved. Finally, habitual or entrenched behavioural patterns can also prompt urges or cravings for drug or alcohol use, owing to their strong conditioned associations with past experiences. This may include an individual visiting old environments such as a local pub where drinking occurred.

Reintroducing useful strategies. Problem-solving techniques provide an effective strategy. In brief, the problem-solving process includes the following steps:

- identify the problem
- generate a range of solutions
- evaluate each solution
- choose the best solution
- decide how to put the solution into action.

Begin this component by exploring with the client his or her plans for the future, and discuss the role that smoking cannabis may or may not have in the achievement or maintenance of these goals. Help the client to beware of rationalizations, as these are an important means by which clients become vulnerable to relapse. Address any possible separation loss or anxiety, such as the feeling of losing a good friend.

Look at ways that the client can continue to monitor progress, to ensure that he or she remains vigilant in the future, particularly during the first few weeks after completing therapy. This can be achieved effectively by having clients record their progress.

Also consider monitoring slips or lapses, and work on strategies that will help the client to deal effectively with setbacks. The client should consider new ways of self-reward, and enjoying drug-free activities.

Finally, help the client to put the changes in a broader context, such as considering other positive lifestyle changes. Looking to the future is an important and appropriate way of concluding therapy for a serious and entrenched problem of drug dependence.

Summary

Until recently cannabis has not been regarded as a drug of dependence. Evidence has emerged in the past few decades that some individuals (perhaps 1 in 10 of those who ever use the drug) can become dependent on it. The number of persons seeking assistance to stop or reduce their cannabis use has increased as the prevalence of cannabis use has increased in the population.

In the absence of extensive clinical experience and clinical research on the treatment of cannabis dependence, the method adopted has been to adapt the CBT approaches used in the treatment of alcohol dependence. The content of such a treatment approach is described. Further research is required into its efficacy.

Opiates 8

Introduction

The opiates (or opioids) include heroin, morphine, codeine, methadone, and pethidine. Opiates are naturally derived from the opium poppy *Papaver somniferum*, which produces a white sap high in natural opiate alkaloids. These alkaloids are extracted to produce the natural opiates heroin and morphine. Research over the past century has yielded synthetic opiates or opioids, such as methadone and pethidine.

Because opiates such as heroin can cause overdose relatively easily, they are viewed as highly dangerous drugs. Their addictive liability is among the highest of all drugs of dependence, after nicotine (Anthony et al., 1994). Because opiates are often injected, their abuse may lead to the transmission of blood-borne diseases such as hepatitis B and C and HIV. The way of life among long-term opiate injectors is often associated with severe physical and psychological harm. In general the dependent use of opiates is among the most damaging of all types of drug dependence. The estimated annual mortality rate among heroin users is around 1%, which is 13 times higher than that among age peers who do not use heroin (English et al., 1995).

Because pure opiates are relatively non-toxic to living tissue and organs, a long-term opiate user given pharmaceutical supplies of pure drug is unlikely to experience the liver, kidney, brain, or lung damage caused by cigarette-smoking and heavy alcohol use. Historically, opiates have been used as powerful analgesics and as treatment for severe diarrhoea, including dysentery. Despite its medical usefulness, heroin has been banned in most Western countries, and the use of morphine is severely restricted to those with terminal illness or overwhelming pain, such as that caused by severe injury.

Assessment

Instruments designed to assess the severity of opioid dependence include the Severity of Opiate Dependence Questionnaire (Sutherland et al., 1986) and the Severity of Dependence Scale (SDS; Gossop et al., 1995). Each instrument is self-administered, and has very good reliability and validity.

The SDS is a brief 5-item instrument that emphasizes the subjective aspects of drug dependence. The questions refer to an individual's concerns about stopping, anxiety regarding missing a dose or hit, and perceived difficulty in stopping using the drug. A cutoff score of 4 (out of a maximum 15) has been established for heroin, amphetamine, and cannabis users (Swift et al., 1998). This instrument has proved to be very useful as a quick and informative measure of the psychological elements of drug dependence, both for research and in clinical practice.

The Opiate Treatment Index (Darke, Ward, Hall, Heather, & Wodak, 1991) is designed to provide a standardized assessment among opiate-using clients. It is a reliable and valid instrument, incorporating basic demographics, treatment history and drug use consumption measures, assessments of HIV risk-taking behaviour, social functioning, criminality, health and psychological adjustment.

Interventions

Detoxification

The opiate withdrawal syndrome is characterized by symptoms such as irritability, anxiety, pain, chills, nausea, diarrhoea, sweating, general weakness, and insomnia. These usually appear 8–12 hours after the last administration of an opiate, peak in intensity at 2–4 days after last use, and largely disappear within 7–10 days. There is a longer-term "secondary" or "protracted abstinence syndrome" of general malaise, decreased well-being, poor tolerance of stress, and a craving for opiates that may last some months during which opioid-dependent persons have a high possibility of relapsing to opiate use.

The opiate withdrawal syndrome is not life threatening. It has been described as "immiserating', and as being like a bout of bad influenza that lasts about a week (Kleber, 1998). It is nonetheless sufficiently aversive for many opiate-dependent persons that it is an obstacle to abstinence that needs to be dealt with humanely and effectively. Detoxification, withdrawal, or cold turkey is experienced very differently by different individuals, as these two examples of withdrawing from heroin show:

> Before my scalded eyes, the paint on the walls starts to shimmer and bubble up. Like boiled vanilla pudding. The whole world's on fire, but the flames are invisible. Their presence apparent only through sheets of heat that waft over the skin. I can't see the flames, only feel them. . . . My skin shines strawberry red. My eyes look dipped in nail polish. (*Stahl* (1996), p. 93)

> Ah need some quickly. The great decline is setting in. It starts as it generally does, with a slight nausea in the pit ay ma stomach and an irrational panic attack. As soon as ah become aware ay the sickness gripping me, it effortlessly moves from the uncomfortable tae the unbearable. A toothache starts tae spread fae ma teeth intae ma jaws and ma eye sockets, and aw through ma bones in a miserable, implacable, debilitating throb. The auld sweat arrives oan cue, and let's no forget the shivers, covering ma back like a thin layer of autumn frost oan a car roof. It's time for action. No way can ah crash oot and face the music yet. Ah need the old "slowburn', a soft, come-down input. The only thing ah can move for is smack. One wee dig tae unravel those twisted limbs and send us oaf tae sleep. Then ah say goodbye to it. (Welsh (1993), pp. 15–16: Withdrawal from heroin)

A number of factors appear to influence rates of completion of opiate detoxification. These include the person's reasons for undertaking detoxification, and the choice of methods available to assist in detoxification. The reasons for requesting detoxification may be mixed: the person may be acting under coercion because he or she face criminal charges; the person may be a stabilized methadone patient who chooses to withdraw from methadone maintenance; the person may intend to reduce the dose of opiate required so that he or she can use opiates at a lower and more affordable dose; or the person may wish to become and remain abstinent.

Methadone-assisted withdrawal is an effective method of achieving opiate withdrawal over a period of a week to 10 days. So, too, is the use of the alpha-adrenergic agonist clonidine. Generally, methadone-assisted withdrawal has been found to be superior to clonidine in rates of completion and experience of withdrawal symptoms, but the two drugs differ in the timing and severity of symptoms. Persons receiving clonidine report more severe withdrawal symptoms early in detoxification when they are most likely to drop out, while methadone patients have fewer symptoms to begin with but report more as the last doses of the drug are withdrawn.

Several studies have found that more patients complete inpatient than outpatient detoxification (Mattick & Hall, 1996). The interpretation of these results is complicated, however, by the fact that the location of detoxification (outpatient or inpatient) has been confounded by the intensity of intervention and support that have typically been greater in the inpatient than in the outpatient setting. It may also be that more opiate- than alcohol-dependent persons live in settings (e.g., with other opiate users) that are unsupportive of detoxification and abstinence, and hence are less likely to complete outpatient detoxification.

Detoxification is *not* a treatment for opiate dependence (Mattick & Hall, 1996). Persons who have undergone detoxification are no less likely to relapse to drug use than those who have not (Gerstein & Harwood, 1990; Simpson & Sells, 1982). In the absence of additional support and treatment most opiate-dependent persons will relapse to opiate use after detoxification (Mattick & Hall, 1996).

Detoxification is more appropriately regarded as a process that aims to achieve a safe and humane withdrawal from a drug of dependence. By this goal, the criteria for assessing its effectiveness are the rates of completion of the process, and the severity of withdrawal symptoms and distress that drug-dependent persons experience. Detoxification also provides opiate-dependent persons with a period of respite from their drug use and its consequences, an occasion to reflect on the wisdom of continued drug use, and an opportunity to take up offers of intervention. Detoxification can thus be a prelude to more specific forms of drug-free treatment for drug dependence.

Drug-free treatment approaches

Drug-free treatment approaches include: residential treatment in Therapeutic Communities (TCs); outpatient drug counselling (DC); and self-help groups such as Narcotics Anonymous (NA). These all share a commitment to achieving abstinence from opioid and other illicit drugs; they do not involve the substitution of other opioid drugs for heroin; and they all use group and psychological interventions to assist dependent heroin users to achieve enduring abstinence and to learn to address their personal problems in ways other than by using opioids.

TCs typically involve residential programmes of 3–12 months in length during which users live and work within a community of other users, ex-users, and professional staff. Group processes and individual counselling are used to change self-defeating behaviour and to support abstinence (Mattick & Hall, 1993). Drug-free outpatient counselling is usually provided individually on an outpatient basis by drug counsellors (usually professionals, but it may include some former drug users). The aim is to address any underlying psychological problems and to assist drug users to become and remain abstinent. These programmes often provide vocational rehabilitation and training.

NA runs self-help groups in the community that follow a programme modelled on the 12-step therapy originally developed by AA. Such programmes are based on the assumption that addiction is a disease for which there is no cure. They assert that recovery can only occur if the addict remains abstinent from all mind-altering substances. The fellowship aims to assist its members to achieve and maintain abstinence by providing mutual help and support in working through the structured programme of the 12 steps.

There is no research evidence on the effectiveness of NA, and there have been no randomized controlled trials for TCs or outpatient DC. Most of the evidence on the effectiveness of TC and DC programmes comes from observational studies such as the Drug Abuse Reporting Program (DARP; Simpson & Sells, 1982) and the Treatment Outcome Prospective Study (TOPS) in the USA (Hubbard, Craddock, Flynn, Anderson, & Etheridge, 1997). In general, TCs and DC are more demanding of drug users, and hence are less successful than methadone maintenance therapy in attracting dependent heroin users into treatment or in retaining them in treatment. TC and DC programmes do achieve substantial reductions in heroin use and crime among the minority of entrants who remain in treatment for long enough to benefit (at least 3 months) (Gerstein & Harwood, 1990; Hubbard et al., 1997; Mattick & Hall, 1993). There is some evidence that TCs may be more effective if they are used in combination with legal coercion or during imprisonment to ensure that heroin users are retained in treatment long enough to benefit from it (Gerstein & Harwood, 1990).

Pharmacotherapies

Because of the low rates of retention and abstinence in drug-free treatment, pharmacotherapies have been used in the treatment of opiate dependence. One of the most widely used of these has been methadone maintenance treatment. Methadone is a synthetic opioid, which has the advantage of being a long-acting opiate that is effective when taken orally. This means that a client of a methadone programme requires only one administration per day, instead of the two or three injections required by a heroin-dependent individual. The oral route of administration also overcomes the risks involved with injecting.

Methadone maintenance was pioneered by Dole and Nyswander in New York in the early 1960s. They argued that opiate addiction was similar to a metabolic illness, such as diabetes. Just as a diabetic requires regular injections of insulin to maintain normal functioning, so opiate addicts required administration of an opiate. Most opiate addicts, they suggested, are either innately or become deficient in endogenous opioids (the natural opiates of the brain, involved in pain regulation). A daily dose of methadone restores this deficiency and maintains the level of opiates at a stable level throughout the period between doses.

While the metabolic theory of opiate dependence has not been supported, the evidence is strongly in favour of methadone as a method of managing opiate dependence (Ward, Mattick, & Hall, 1998). Methadone maintenance treatment has been shown to reduce heroin use, infectious disease transmission, damage to veins and skin infections, criminal activity, psychological problems, and social problems (Ward et al., 1998). Methadone does not entirely eliminate the illicit use of opiates, nor the use of other illicit drugs, such as cocaine and cannabis, which are abused by methadone clients, but illicit opiate and other drugs are substantially reduced by methadone maintenance treatment (Ward et al., 1998).

Methadone maintenance is a well-accepted intervention for opioid dependence, and is widely used in Australia (Ward et al., 1998), the USA, and the UK. At present it is the most effective intervention for individuals suffering from heroin dependence (see Ward et al., 1998 for a review of the evidence and issues surrounding its use). It is common that people who are dependent on heroin have an improved quality of life when taking methadone:

> A 24-year-old single woman presents for treatment for her heroin problem. Two weeks before she had been

disciplined and given notice in her job due to lateness. She was resolved to keep her job. She began a methadone programme and after an initial period of daily attendance for dose titration, she was stabilized on methadone.

Alternative maintenance treatments

Levo-alpha-acetylmethadol

Levo-alpha-acetylmethadol (LAAM) is a synthetic opiate agonist with an action that is similar to morphine, but has a much longer half-life than that of other opiates; its duration of action lies between 48 and 72 hours. Its extensive action means that dosing is only necessary three times a week and the safety and efficacy of LAAM is similar to the profile of methadone. The VA Cooperative study, examining the comparative effectiveness of LAAM and methadone (Ling, Charuvastra, Kaim, & Klett, 1976), found that more subjects in the LAAM group (80 mg three times a week) dropped out of treatment compared to the low dose (50 mg daily) or high dose (100 mg daily) methadone groups. However, for those who stayed in the study, the efficacy of LAAM was similar to high-dose methadone, and superior to low-dose methadone.

Studies have also assessed the feasibility of moving patients from methadone to LAAM: a greater proportion of methadone patients dropped out compared to those who crossed over to LAAM, and more patients opted to continue LAAM maintenance compared to methadone patients.

The advantages of LAAM in comparison to methadone lie in the relatively slower onset of the effects, and in the longer duration of the action. This has two consequences: the risks of abuse by patients are reduced as the effects are not felt immediately, which results in a lower risk of LAAM being diverted for abuse by persons not enrolled in LAAM maintenance. Second, it also requires fewer visits for dosing, making fewer demands on both the patients and on the service provider, resulting in greater flexibility for the client and concomitant reductions in dose preparation and record-keeping on the part of clinics.

Buprenorphine

Buprenorphine is a mixed agonist–antagonist: it has partial agonist effects similar to those of morphine, but blocks the effects of pure agonists such as heroin or morphine. When given in high doses, the effects of buprenorphine can last for up to 3 days (Oliveto & Kosten, 1997). An attractive feature of buprenorphine is the antagonist effect that is seen at higher doses, which has important implications in the risk of overdose and abuse potential (Oliveto & Kosten, 1997). The optimal dosage of buprenorphine is yet to be determined but research has found that doses of 8 mg daily result in similar rates of opiate-free urine screens to methadone doses of 60 mg daily (Johnson, Jaffe, & Fudala, 1992). Because of the long half-life of buprenorphine, dosing may be made on an alternate or thrice-daily basis, which results in increased flexibility for the client and reduced demands on the clinic.

Naltrexone

Naltrexone has been used as an opiate antagonist for a number of decades. It is a complete opiate antagonist that blocks the opiate receptor cells so that any opiates in a person's system will be displaced, meaning that if any opiates are taken, they have no effect. Naltrexone maintenance hence aims to ensure that the client remains opiate-free.

A central requirement for the effectiveness of naltrexone maintenance is that the treatment is taken daily: hence, one of the biggest determinants of the effectiveness of naltrexone's efficacy is the client's motivation to remain abstinent (and therefore to take naltrexone). Such motivation may not characterize the majority of opiate-dependent persons, many of whom enter treatment through coercion (either legal or social); indeed, research has shown that 90% of individuals on naltrexone maintenance resume illicit opiate use within 12 months in the absence of outpatient treatment (Kosten, 1990).

The success of naltrexone maintenance, as for any treatment, depends on the type of treatment programme and the nature of the client group (Stine & Kosten, 1997). For example, research indicates that the majority of business executives and physicians who are opiate dependent and are prescribed naltrexone in combination with outpatient treatment and therapy will significantly improve their social and professional functioning (which was disrupted secondary to their opiate dependence), and most will remain opiate-free (Gold, Dackis, & Washton, 1984; Ling & Wesson, 1984; Roth, Hogan, & Farren, 1997; Washton, Gold, & Pottash, 1984). In comparison, a study carried out in a suburban health project clinic with opiate-dependent persons with an average length of 10.5 years of dependence found that after 90 days, only 17% of clients remained in treatment, despite the fact that they all expressed a desire for abstinence-based treatment (Rawson & Tennant, 1984).

Summary

The opiates have the highest dependence potential of psychoactive drugs after nicotine. Heroin dependence is one of the most serious types of drug dependence in terms of its persistence, its mortality rate, and the substantial psychological and physical morbidity experienced by heroin-dependent persons.

Completion of opiate withdrawal is not life threatening but it can be immiserating and an obstacle to the achievement of abstinence. Opiate withdrawal can be completed using methadone or clonidine. Detoxification is not a treatment for opiate dependence. Without follow-up treatment and support most heroin-dependent persons return to heroin use after completing withdrawal.

Drug-free forms of treatment that aim to achieve enduring abstinence from treatment include TCs, drug-free counselling, and self-help groups such as NA. Drug-free approaches are not attractive to many users and have modest rates of retention, but are of considerable benefit to the minority of patients who remain in them long enough to benefit from them (3 months or more).

The major form of treatment for opiate dependence in Australia, the UK, and the USA has been methadone maintenance treatment. This involves maintaining heroin-dependent persons on the long-acting oral opioid methadone, usually given daily under supervision. This stabilizes the person's opiate use and makes him or her more accessible to psychological and social interventions. It has been shown to substantially reduce heroin use and crime and to improve the health and well-being of heroin-dependent persons.

In the interests of increasing patient choice and the attractiveness of treatment, a number of alternative maintenance agents have been investigated. These include LAAM, a longer-acting form of methadone, buprenorphine (a mixed agonist–antagonist drug), and naltrexone, a pure opioid antagonist. LAAM and buprenorphine produce approximately comparable outcomes to methadone treatment. Naltrexone has much lower rates of retention but may be of use in selected patients in whom compliance can be supervised, such as opioid-dependent health professionals.

Psychostimulants: amphetamines and cocaine 9

Introduction

Evidence from a number of countries, including the USA, the UK, Australia, and countries in Europe (Klee, 1992), indicates that illicit amphetamine use re-emerged among young adults in the early 1990s. Unlike an earlier epidemic of illicit amphetamine use in the early 1970s, the 1990s' epidemic has included widespread experimentation with injection as a route of administration (Klee, 1992). The main drugs in this group are amphetamine sulphate and methamphetamine.

The apparent increase in the prevalence of injecting amphetamines raises a number of health concerns. First, sharing of injecting equipment by amphetamine users and unsafe sexual practices may transmit HIV and other serious infectious diseases such as hepatitis C. Amphetamine users are younger than opioid users, more sexually active, and may engage in higher levels of unsafe sexual behaviour, which may be facilitated by the pharmacological effects of amphetamines (Hando, Topp, & Hall, 1997; Klee, 1992).

Second, chronic, heavy use of amphetamines by injection carries specific health risks. Acutely, large doses can sometimes lead to fatal overdoses, with cardiac arrhythmias, hypothermia, convulsions, and cerebral infarct as causes of death (Hando et al., 1997). Chronic, heavy use can lead to a dependence syndrome with a high risk of relapse to use, and to a paranoid psychosis (Hando et al., 1997). Users can become aggressive and violent while experiencing persecutory auditory hallucinations and delusions (Gawin & Kleber, 1986).

Assessment

A non-confrontational, empathic, and mutually respectful therapeutic relationship is more likely to engage those more entrenched patients who are unwilling to accept that they have a problem (Platt, 1997). In the assessment of patients, the therapist should obtain the patient's history of drug use, including where, how, and why the stimulant has been used. It should also involve obtaining a psychiatric history and any information that relates psychiatric ill-health to such use. Finally, it should include a thorough physical examination, including urinalysis.

Standard self-report questionnaires are available that have been designed specifically for the assessment of cocaine abuse. The Voris Cocaine Craving Scale (Smelson, McGee, Caulfield, Bergstein, & Engelhart, 1999) and the Drug Impairment Rating Scale (Halikas, Crosby, & Nugent, 1992; Halikas, Nugent, Crosby, & Carlson, 1993) have both been shown to have good reliability and validity for assessing self-reported impairment both for assessment and treatment outcome measurement purposes. Kampman et al. (1998) developed the Cocaine Selective Severity Assessment (CSSA) – a scale to measure the symptoms of early cocaine withdrawal. They found the instrument clinically useful, especially in predicting early treatment failure, and presented evidence of good reliability and validity in their report.

There are also general addiction measures that have been found to be useful for the assessment of cocaine dependence prior to treatment. For example, standard measures of readiness to change (Barnes & Samet, 1997; Prochaska & DiClemente, 1986) may assist the clinician to establish patients' presenting attitudes towards their drug problems as well as provide a basis for motivating change behaviour.

Interventions

Expert reviews (Bigelow & Walsh, 1998; Platt, 1997; Tutton & Crayton, 1993) have classified pharmacotherapies for cocaine abuse into four broad categories: (1) drugs that treat pre-morbid coexisting psychiatric disorders; (2) drugs that treat cocaine withdrawal and craving; (3) cocaine antagonists that block the action of cocaine; and (4) drugs that cause an aversive reaction to cocaine. One further category, raised by Kaminiencki et al. in their review of interventions and care for psychostimulant users, is that of stimulant replacement therapy (Kamieniecki, Vincent, Allsop, & Lintzeris, 1998).

In his review of treatments for stimulant dependence, Schuckit (1994) concluded that no pharmacological intervention had been found to be superior to placebo for the treatment of stimulant-dependent individuals. However, there has been an increase in research since then, with most of the research on treatments for psychostimulant abuse disorders being carried out on cocaine and in the USA. There is little specific research available on treatments for amphetamine abuse.

Detoxification

Detoxification from cocaine appears to have relatively low-level withdrawal symptoms. In a recent review of the literature, it was *not* recommended that medication be used to assist patients (Proudfoot & Teesson, 2000).

Pharmacotherapies

There is some evidence that fluoxetine (Prozac) may be of use in treatment, particularly among persons who also have problematic opiate use, although further controlled research on this is required (Proudfoot & Teesson, 2000). Other antidepressants appear to have little efficacy in the treatment of cocaine dependence. Desipramine does not appear to be an effective pharmacotherapy for cocaine dependence, despite early potential for efficacy (Proudfoot & Teesson, 2000).

There has been no research showing that any pharmacological interventions are effective for persons with amphetamine dependence (Proudfoot & Teesson, 2000). As a harm minimization approach, amphetamine substitution may be of use, and psychosocial interventions have been recommended to complement any pharmacological intervention for amphetamine-dependent persons (Proudfoot & Teesson, 2000).

Cognitive behavioural techniques

Recent research suggests that cognitive behavioural techniques may be of use, particularly in the form of therapy that addresses coping skills and deals with risky drug-taking situations. There is evidence that more intensive programmes (at least one session per week) may be more effective (Proudfoot & Teesson, 2000), and research suggests that a minimum of 3 months may be needed to complete such therapy.

There have been no published studies of the efficacy of such treatment for amphetamine dependence. Contingency management and cognitive behavioural therapy that incorporates relapse prevention have been recommended as the most appropriate therapies.

Summary

There is now a considerable body of research on cocaine abuse, but a paucity of good research on assessment and treatments for amphetamine abuse; there is also a need for greater recognition of the prevalence and harm associated with amphetamine abuse. Further research on pharmacotherapies for cocaine (and other stimulants) needs to include complementary psychosocial therapies and demonstrate that specific pharmacotherapies add to overall treatment effectiveness. The safety of psychostimulant use is unpredictable and, given the poor retention rates achieved in this area of research, caution should be exercised when trialling new medications owing to the possibility of additive negative effects of the trial drug and the psychostimulant. Treatments for amphetamine abuse have been poorly researched and no pharmacological interventions have yet been found to be effective. One possible area of research is the use of replacement medication based on harm minimization principles. Other pharmacotherapies may emerge once there is appropriate recognition of the extent of the problem.

Addiction: The highs and lows 10

What are the current controversies in the addictions and where should our efforts in research and understanding be directed? At the beginning of this book we set out to answer two questions:

- *Why do some people develop problems with alcohol and drugs and others do not?*
- *How do we respond?*

These are complex and intriguing questions with no simple answers as addiction is determined by a multiple of interacting factors, and it is the unravelling of these factors that presents the challenge for the future.

There is little doubt that the addictions cause a considerable burden to society. The Global Burden of Disease study confirmed that alcohol was a major contributor to the burden of disease in developed countries, and as a risk factor for injury and alcohol dependence (Murray & Lopez, 1996). Yet, the extent of the burden remains to be clearly outlined for all drugs. This is probably more so for cannabis than for any other drug. Controversy remains about the health consequences with a 10-year study of 65,171 Kaiser Permanente Medical Care Program members finding that regular marijuana use had little impact on mortality (Sidney, Beck, & Tekawa, 1997). Such reassurance about the mortality risks of marijuana is premature because the mean age at follow-up was only 43 years; and cigarette-smoking and alcohol use were only modestly associated with pre-mature mortality. The health consequences of cannabis is a continuing debate in the addictions.

In alcohol dependence, treatment effects remain modest. The debate as to whether treatment should be matched to patient charac-teristics and thus improve this modest effect is as yet unresolved.

However, Project MATCH (Matching Alcoholism Treatments to Client Heterogeneity; Project MATCH Research Group, 1997) questioned the hope that the modest benefits of psychosocial treatment of alcohol dependence could be improved by matching patients to type of treatment. Over 1,000 alcohol-dependent patients received carefully implemented forms of three competing psychosocial treatments (motivational enhancement, cognitive behaviour, and 12-step facilitation). The 10 variables that previous research indicated may interact with treatment were measured. Only psychiatric disorder interacted with treatment outcome. To the surprise of supporters of these treatment approaches, outcome at 12 months was equally good for the three treatments.

The illegality of some drugs of addiction will continue to present both moral and logistical issues in our response. In particular, the use of illicit drugs for the treatment of dependence remains both an ethical and logistical challenge in the addictions. The availability of injectable heroin for the heroin dependent was recently tested in trials on 1,100 Swiss, heroin-dependent patients in whom all previous treatments had failed. The study showed that the prescription of injectable heroin under medical supervision and with intensive medical, psychological, and social support, reduced self-reported use of heroin and other drugs, criminal activity, and involvement in the drug scene (Uchtenhagen-Gutzwiller & Dobler-Mikola, 1997). Participants' health and social adjustment also substantially improved. In a subsequent referendum the Swiss voted to continue heroin prescription.

What of the future? A growing understanding of the neurobiology of alcohol and drug addiction may lead to new and better pharmacological treatments of alcohol and other drug dependence. The recent increase in the use of illicit drugs by young Americans will probably prompt investment in basic science and efforts to translate advances into effective treatment. The challenge is to incorporate new pharmacological treatments within a public-health approach to alcohol and other drug use. A combination of biological and social perspectives on drug use and addiction is required if we are substantially to reduce the burden of disease and disability produced by alcohol and other drug use (Hall, 1997).

References

Abbot, N.C., Stead, L.F., White, A.R., Barnes, J., & Ernst, E. (2000). Hypnotherapy for smoking cessation. *Cochrane Database of Systematic Reviews, 2*.

Adams, I., & Martin, B. (1996). Cannabis: Pharmacology and toxicology in animals and humans. *Addiction, 91* (11), 1585–1614.

Agency for Health Care Policy and Research. (1996). Smoking cessation clinical practice guideline: The smoking cessation clinical practice guideline for panel and staff. *Journal of the American Medical Association, 275*, 1270–1280.

Ainslie, G. (1992). *Picoeconomics*. Cambridge: Cambridge University Press.

Alterman, A.I., Hayashida, M., & O'Brien, C.P. (1988). Treatment response and safety of ambulatory medical detoxication. *Journal of Studies on Alcohol, 49* (2), 160–166.

Altman, J., Everitt, B., Glautier, S., Markou, A., Nutt, D., Oretti, R., Phillips, G., & Robbins, T. (1996). The biological, social and clinical bases of drug addiction: Commentary and debate. *Psychopharmacology, 125*, 285–345.

American Psychiatric Association. (1987). *Diagnostic and statistical manual of mental disorders* (3rd ed., rev.). Washington, DC: American Psychiatric Association.

American Psychiatric Association. (1994). *Diagnostic and statistical manual of mental disorders* (4th ed.). Washington, DC: American Psychiatric Association.

Anda, R., Williamson, D., Escobedo, L., Mast, E., Giovino, G., & Remington, P. (1990). Depression and the dynamics of smoking. *Journal of the American Medical Association, 264* (12), 1541–1545.

Annis, H.M., & Graham, J.M. (1988). *Situational Confidence Questionnaire (SCQ): Users' guide*. Toronto: ARF.

Anthony, J.C., Warner, L., & Kessler, R. (1994). Comparative epidemiology of dependence on tobacco, alcohol, controlled substances, and inhalants: Basic findings from the National Comorbidity Survey. *Experimental and Clinical Psychopharmacology, 2* (3), 244–268.

Australian Bureau of Statistics. (1998). *National Survey of Mental Health and Wellbeing of Adults: Users' guide*. Canberra: Australian Bureau of Statistics.

Azrin, N.H., Acierno, R., Kogan, E.S., Donohue, B., Besalel, V.A., & McMahon, P.T. (1996). Follow-up results of supportive versus behavioral therapy for illicit drug use. *Behaviour Research & Therapy, 34* (1), 41–46.

Babor, T.F. (1994). Avoiding the horrid and beastly sin of drunkenness: Does dissuasion make a difference? *Journal of Consulting and Clinical Psychology, 62* (6), 1127–1140.

Babor, T.F., Orrock, B., Liebowitz, N., Salomon, R., & Brown, J. (1990). From basic concepts to clinical reality: Unresolved issues in the diagnosis of dependency. In M. Galanter (Ed.), *Recent developments in alcoholism* (pp. 85–109). New York: Plenum Press.

Bammer, G., Ostini, R., & Sengoz, A. (1995). Using ambulance service records to examine nonfatal heroin overdoses. *Australian Journal of Public Health*, 19, 316–317.

Barnes, H.N., & Samet, J.H. (1997). Brief interventions with substance-abusing patients. *Medical Clinics of North America*, 81 (4), 867–879.

Barrett, J.E., & Witkin, J.M. (1986). The role of behavioral and pharmacological history in determining the effects of abused drugs. In S.R. Goldberg & I. Stolerman (Eds.), *Behavioral analysis of drug dependence* (pp. 195–224). Orlando: Academic Press.

Baucom, D.H., Mueser, K.T., Daiuto, A.D., & Stickle, T.R. (1998). Empirically supported couple and family interventions for marital distress and adult mental health problems. *Journal of Consulting and Clinical Psychology*, 66 (1), 53–88.

Beck, A.T., & Steer, R.A. (1987). *Beck Depression Inventory: Manual*. USA: Harcourt, Brace, Jovanovich.

Beck, A.T., & Steer, R.A. (1990). *Beck Anxiety Inventory: Manual*. USA: Harcourt, Brace, Jovanovich.

Becker, G.S., & Murphy, K.M. (1988). A theory of rational addiction. *Journal of Political Economy*, 96, 675–700.

Benowitz, N., & Gourlay, S.G. (1997). Cardiovascular toxicity of nicotine: Implications for nicotine replacement therapy. *Journal of the American College of Cardiologists*, 29, 1422–1431.

Benowitz, N.L. (1998). Nicotine pharmacology and addiction. In N.L. Benowitz (Ed.), *Nicotine safety and toxicity* (pp. 3–18). New York: Oxford University Press.

Bergman, J., Kamien, J., & Spealman, R. (1990). Antagonism of cocaine self-administration by selective dopamine D1 and D2 antagonists. *Behavioral Pharmacology*, 1, 355–363.

Bierut, L.J., Dinwiddie, S.H., Begleiter, H., Crowe, R.R., Hesselbrock, V., Nurnberger, J.I., Porjesz, B., Schuckit, M.A., & Reich, T. (1998). Familial transmission of substance dependence: Alcohol, marijuana, cocaine, and habitual smoking. A report from the Collaborative Study on the Genetics of Alcoholism. *Archives of General Psychiatry*, 55 (11), 982–988.

Bigelow, G.E., & Walsh, S.L. (1998). Evaluation of potential pharmacotherapies: Response to cocaine challenge in the human laboratory. In S.T. Higgins & J.L. Katz (Eds.), *Cocaine abuse: behavior, pharmacology, and clinical applications*. San Diego: Academic Press.

Bohman, M., Sigvardsson, S., & Cloninger, R. (1981). Maternal inheritance of alcohol abuse: Cross-fostering analysis of adopted women. *Archives of General Psychiatry*, 38, 965–969.

Brook, J.S., Whiteman, M., Gordon, A., & Brook, D. (1988). The role of older brothers in younger brothers' drug use viewed in the context of parent and peer influences. *Journal of Genetic Psychology*, 151, 59–75.

Brown, R.A., Evans, D.M., Miller, I.W., Burgess, E.S., & Mueller, T.I. (1997). Cognitive-behavioral treatment for depression in alcoholism. *Journal of Consulting and Clinical Psychology*, 65 (5), 715–726.

Budney, A.J., Bickel, W.K., & Amass, L. (1998). Marijuana use and treatment outcome among opioid-dependent patients. *Addiction*, 93 (4), 493–503.

Caine, S., & Koob, G. (1994). Effects of dopamine D1 and D2 antagonists on cocaine self-administration under different schedules of reinforcement in the rat. *Journal of Pharmacology Experimental Therapy*, 270, 209–218.

Center for Disease Control and Prevention. (1992). Comparison of the cigarette brand preferences of adult and teenage smokers: US, 1989, and ten US communities, 1988 and 1990. *Mortality and Morbidity Weekly Report, 41*, 169–173.

Chaisson, R.E., Osmond, D., Brodie, B., Sande, M.A., & Moss, A.R. (1989). Cocaine use and HIV infection in intravenous drug users in San Francisco. *Journal of the American Medical Association, 261* (4), 561–565.

Cherpitel, C.J. (1995). Analysis of cut points for screening instruments for alcohol problems in the emergency room. *Journal of Studies on Alcohol, 56* (6), 695–700.

Chick, J., Lloyd, G., & Crombie, E. (1985). Counselling problem drinkers in medical wards: A controlled study. *British Medical Journal, 290*, 965–967.

Cicchetti, D., & Rogosch, F.A. (1999). Psychopathology as risk for adolescent substance use disorders: A developmental psychopathology perspective. *Journal of Clinical Child Psychology, 28* (3), 355–365.

Cloninger, R., Bohman, M., & Sigvardsson, S. (1981). Inheritance of alcohol abuse: Cross fostering analysis of adopted men. *Archives of General Psychiatry, 38*, 861–868.

Collins, D., & Lapsley, H. (1996). *The social costs of drug abuse in Australia*. Canberra: Australian Government Publishing Service.

Comings, D.E., Muhleman, D., Gade, R., Johnson, P., Verde, R., Saucier, G., & MacMurray, J. (1997). Cannabinoid receptor gene (CNR1): Association with i.v. drug use. *Molecular Psychiatry, 2* (2), 161–168.

Conigrave, K.M., Hall, W.D., & Saunders, J.B. (1995). The AUDIT questionnaire: Choosing a cut-off score. *Addiction, 90* (10), 1349–1356.

Costello, E., Erkanli, A., Federman, E., & Angold, A. (1999). Development of psychiatric comorbidity with substance abuse in adolescents: Effects of timing and sex. *Journal of Clinical Child Psychology, 28* (3), 298–311.

Cottler, L.B., Phelps, D.L., & Crompton, W.M. (1995). Narrowing of the drinking repertoire criterion: Should it have been dropped from ICD-10? *Journal of Studies on Alcohol, 56*, 173–176.

Crofts, N., Hopper, J., Bowden, D., Beschkin, A., Milner, R., & Locarnini, S. (1993). Hepatitis C infection among a cohort of Victorian injecting drug users. *Medical Journal of Australia, 159*, 237–241.

Darke, S., Baker, A., Dixon, J., Wodak, A., & Heather, N. (1992). Drug use and HIV risk-taking behaviour among clients in methadone maintenance treatment. *Drug and Alcohol Dependence, 29* (3), 263–268.

Darke, S., Hall, W., Kaye, S., Ross, J., & DeFlou, J. (2000a). *Hair morphine concentrations of fatal heroin overdose cases and living heroin users* (Technical Report 90). Sydney, Australia: National Drug and Alcohol Research Centre, UNSW.

Darke, S., Hall, W., Weatherburn, D., & Lind, B. (1999). Fluctuations in heroin purity and the incidence of fatal heroin overdose. *Drug and Alcohol Dependence, 54* (2), 155–161.

Darke, S., & Ross, J. (1997a). Overdose risk perceptions and behaviours among heroin users in Sydney, Australia. *European Addiction Research, 3* (2), 87–92.

Darke, S., & Ross, J. (1997b). Polydrug dependence and psychiatric comorbidity among heroin injectors. *Drug and Alcohol Dependence, 48* (2), 135–141.

Darke, S., Ross, J., & Hall, W. (1996a). Overdose among heroin users in Sydney, Australia: I. Prevalence and correlates of non-fatal overdose. *Addiction, 91* (3), 405–411.

Darke, S., Ross, J., & Hall, W. (1996b). Overdose among heroin users in Sydney, Australia: II. Responses to overdose. *Addiction, 91* (3), 413–417.

Darke, S., Ross, J., Zador, D., & Sunjic, S. (2000b). Heroin-related deaths in New South Wales, Australia 1992–1996. *Drug and Alcohol Dependence, 60,* 141–150.

Darke, S., Ward, J., Hall, W., Heather, N., & Wodak, A. (1991). *The opiate treatment index (OTI) manual* (Technical Report 11). Sydney, Australia: National Drug and Alcohol Research Centre, UNSW.

Darke, S., & Zador, D. (1996). Fatal heroin "overdose": A review. *Addiction, 91* (12), 1765–1772.

Davidson, D. (1985). Deception and division. In J. Elster (Ed.), *The multiple self.* Cambridge: Cambridge University Press.

Davies, D.L. (1962). Normal drinking in recovered alcohol addicts. *Quarterly Journal of Studies on Alcohol, 21,* 94–104.

Derlet, R.W., Rice, P., Horowitz, B.Z., & Lord, R.V. (1989). Amphetamine toxicity: Experience with 127 cases. *Journal of Emergency Medicine, 7* (2), 157–161.

Derogatis, L.R. (1983). *SCL-90R: Administration, Scoring and Procedures Manual – II for the Revised Version.* Towson, MD, USA: Clinical Psychometric Research.

Di Chiara, G., & North, R.A. (1992). Neurobiology of opiate abuse. *Trends in Pharmacological Science, 13,* 185–193.

Diaz, R., & Fruhauf, A. (1991). The origins and development of self-regulation: A developmental model on the risk for addictive behaviours. In N. Heather, W. Miller, & J. Greeley (Eds.), *Self-control and the addictive behaviours* (pp. 83–106). Sydney: Maxwell Macmillan Publishing Australia.

Didcott, P., Reilly, D., Swift, W., & Hall, W. (1997). *Long-term cannabis users on the New South Wales coast* (Technical Report 30). Sydney, Australia: National Drug and Alcohol Research Centre, UNSW.

Dinwiddie, S.H., Cottler, L., Compton, W., & Abdallah, A.B. (1996). Psychopathology and HIV risk behaviors among injection drug users in and out of treatment. *Drug and Alcohol Dependence, 43* (1–2), 1–11.

Drummond, D.C. (1997). Alcohol interventions: Do the best things come in small packages? *Addiction, 92* (4), 375–379.

Drummond, D.C., Tiffany, S., Glautier, S., & Remington, B. (1995). Cue exposure in understanding and treating addictive behaviours. In D.C. Drummond, S. Tiffany, S. Glautier, & B. Remington (Eds.), *Addictive behaviour: Cue exposure theory and practice* (pp. 1–17). Chichester: John Wiley & Sons Ltd.

Edwards, G., Anderson, P., Babor, T.F., Casswell, S., Ferrence, R., Giesbrecht, N., Godfrey, C., Holder, H.D., Lemmens, P., Makela, K., Midanik, L.T., Norstrom, T., Osterberg, E., Romelsjo, A., Room, R., Simpura, J., & Skog, O.J. (1994). *Alcohol policy and public good.* Oxford: Oxford University Press.

Edwards, G., Arif, A., & Hodgson, R. (1981). Nomenclature and classification of drug and alcohol related problems: A WHO memorandum. *Bulletin of the World Health Organization, 50,* 225–242.

Edwards, G., & Gross, M.M. (1976). Alcohol dependence: Provisional description of clinical syndrome. *British Medical Journal, 1,* 1058–1061.

Edwards, G., Gross, M.M., Keller, M., Moser, J., & Room, R. (1977). *Alcohol related disabilities* (Offset Publication 32). Geneva, Switzerland: World Health Organization.

Eley, T.C., & Plomin, R. (1997). Genetic analyses of emotionality. *Current Opinion in Neurobiology, 7* (2), 279–284.

Elster, J., & Skog, O.J. (Eds.). (1999). *Getting hooked: Rationality and addiction.*

Cambridge: Cambridge University Press.

Elvy, G.A., Wells, J.E., & Baird, K.A. (1988). Attempted referral as intervention for problem drinking in the general hospital. *British Journal of Addiction, 83,* 83–89.

English, D., Holman, C.D.J., Milne, E., Winter, M.G., Hulse, G.K., Codde, J.P., Corti, B., Dawes, V., de Klerk, N., Knuiman, M.W., Kurinczuk, J.J., Lewin, G.F., & Ryan, G.A. (1995). *The quantification of drug caused morbidity and mortality in Australia.* Canberra, Australia: Commonwealth Department of Human Services and Health.

Environmental Protection Agency. (1992). *Respiratory health effects of passive smoking: Lung cancers and other disorders.* Washington: Office of Air and Radiation, US Environmental Protection Agency.

European Monitoring Centre for Drugs and Drug Addiction. (1998). *Annual report on the state of the drugs problem in the European Union.* Lisbon: European Monitoring Centre for Drugs and Drug Addiction.

Eysenck, H. (1997). Addiction, personality and motivation. *Human Psychopharmacology, 12,* s79–s87.

Eysenck, H.J., & Eysenck, M.W. (1985). *Personality and individual differences.* New York: Plenum Press.

Fergusson, D.M., & Horwood, L.J. (1997). Early onset cannabis use and psychosocial adjustment in young adults. *Addiction, 92* (3), 279–296.

Fiore, M., Bailey, W., & Cohen, S. (1996). *Smoking cessation* (AHCPR publication no. 96-0692). Rockville: US Department of Health and Human Services, Public Health Service, Agency for Health Care Policy and Research.

Fiore, M., Smith, S., Jorenby, D., & Baker, T. (1994). The effectiveness of the nicotine patch for smoking cessation: A meta-analysis. *Journal of the American Medical Association, 271* (24), 1940–1947.

Flaherty, B., Homel, P., & Hall, W. (1991). Public attitudes towards alcohol control policies. *Australian Journal of Public Health, 15* (4), 301–306.

Fleming, M.F. (1993). Screening and brief intervention for alcohol disorders. *Journal of Family Practice, 37* (3), 231–234.

Fleming, M.F., Barry, K.L., Manwell, L.B., Johnson, K., & London, R. (1997). Brief physician advice for problem alcohol drinkers: A randomized controlled trial in community-based primary care practices. *Journal of the American Medical Association, 277* (13), 1039–1045.

Francis, L. (1996). The relationship between Eysenck's personality factors and attitude towards substance use among 13-15 year olds. *Personality and Individual Differences, 21* (5), 633–640.

Gardner, E.L. (1992). Cannabinoid interaction with brain reward systems – the neurobiological basis of cannabinoid abuse. In L. Murphy & A. Bartke (Eds.), *Marijuana/cannabinoids: Neurobiology and neurophysiology.* London: CRC Press.

Gawin, F.H., & Kleber, H.D. (1986). Abstinence symptomatology and psychiatric diagnosis in cocaine abusers: Clinical observations. *Archives of General Psychiatry, 43* (2), 107–113.

Gerstein, D.R., & Harwood, H. (1990). *Treating drug problems. Volume 1: A study of effectiveness and financing of public and private drug treatment systems.* Washington: National Academy Press.

Gilbert, D.G., & Gilbert, B.O. (1995). Personality, psychopathology and nicotine response as mediators of the genetics of smoking. *Behavior Genetics, 25* (2), 133–147.

Gittelman, R., Mannuzza, S., Shenker, R., & Bonagura, N. (1985). Hyperactive boys almost grown up: I. Psychiatric status. *Archives of General Psychiatry*, *42*, 937–947.

Gold, M.S., Dackis, C.A., & Washton, A.M. (1984). The sequential use of clonidine and naltrexone in the treatment of opiate addicts. *Advances in Alcohol and Substance Abuse, 3* (3), 19–39.

Goodwin, D., Schulsinger, R., Hermansen, L., Guze, S., & Winokur, G. (1973). Alcohol problems in adoptees raised apart from biological parents. *Archives of General Psychiatry, 28*, 238–255.

Gossop, M., Darke, S., Griffiths, P., Hando, J., Powis, B., Hall, W., & Strang, J. (1995). The severity of dependence scale (SDS): Psychometric properties of the SDS in English and Australian samples of heroin, cocaine and amphetamine users. *Addiction, 90*, 607–614.

Gossop, M., Griffiths, P., Powis, B., Williamson, S., & Strang, J. (1996). Frequency of non-fatal heroin overdose: Survey of heroin users recruited in non-clinical settings. *British Medical Journal, 313*, 402.

Gourlay, S. (1994). The pros and cons of transdermal nicotine therapy. *Medical Journal of Australia, 160*, 152–159.

Gowing, L.R., Ali, R.L., & White, J.M. (2000). *Respiratory harms of smoked cannabis* (Monograph 8). Sydney: Drug and Alcohol Services Council.

Greeley, J., Swift, W., & Heather, N. (1992). Depressed affect as a predictor of increased desire for alcohol in current drinkers of alcohol. *British Journal of Addiction, 87* (7), 1005–1012.

Greeley, J., & Westbrook, F. (1991). Associative learning, drug use and addictive behaviour. In N. Heather, W. Miller, & J. Greeley (Eds.), *Self-control and the addictive behaviours* (pp. 127–152). Sydney: Maxwell Macmillan Publishing Australia.

Grenyer, B.F.S., Laborsky, L., & Solowij, N. (1995). *Treatment manual for suppportive–expressive dynamic psychotherapy: Special adaptation for treatment of cannabis*

(marijuana) dependence. Sydney, Australia: National Drug and Alcohol Research Centre, UNSW.

Hajek, P., & Stead, L.F. (2000). Aversive smoking for smoking cessation. *Cochrane Database of Systematic Reviews, 2*.

Halikas, J.A., Crosby, R.D., & Nugent, S.M. (1992). The convergent validity of the Drug Impairment Rating Scale for Cocaine. *Psychopharmacology Bulletin, 28* (3), 315–318.

Halikas, J.A., Nugent, S.M., Crosby, R.D., & Carlson, G.A. (1993). 1990–1991 survey of pharmacotherapies used in the treatment of cocaine abuse. *Journal of Addictive Diseases, 12* (2), 129–139.

Hall, S., Reus, V., Munoz, R., Sees, K., Humfleet, G., Hartz, D., Frederick, S., & Triffleman, S. (1998a). Nortriptyline and cognitive-behavioral therapy in the treatment of cigarette smoking. *Archives of General Psychiatry, 55* (8), 683–690.

Hall, W. (1996). What have population surveys revealed about substance use disorders and their co-morbidity with other mental disorders? *Drug and Alcohol Review, 15*, 157–170.

Hall, W. (1997). Addiction: Highs and lows. *Lancet, 350*, Suppl. 3: S1111.

Hall, W. (1998). Cannabis use and psychosis. *Drug and Alcohol Review, 17*, 433–444.

Hall, W., & Hando, J. (1993). Amphetamine use as a public health problem in Australia. *Medical Journal of Australia, 159* (10), 643–644.

Hall, W., Johnston, L., & Donnelly, N. (1999a). Epidemiology of cannabis use and its consequences. In H. Kalant, W. Corrigall, W. Hall, & R. Smart (Eds.), *The health effects of cannabis* (pp. 71–125). Toronto, Canada: Centre for Addiction and Mental Health.

Hall, W., Lynskey, M., & Degenhardt, L. (1999b). *Heroin use in Australia: Its impact on public health and public order*

(Monograph 42). Sydney: National Drug and Alcohol Research Centre.

Hall, W., & Solowij, N. (1998). Adverse effects of cannabis. *Lancet*, *352*, 1611–1616.

Hall, W., Solowij, N., & Lemon, J. (1994). *The health and psychological consequences of cannabis use*. Sydney: National Drug and Alcohol Research Centre.

Hall, W., Teesson, M., Lynskey, M., & Degenhardt, L. (1999c). The prevalence in the past year of substance use and ICD-10 substance use disorders in Australian adults: Findings from the national survey of mental health and well-being. *Addictions* (in press).

Hall, W., Teesson, M., Lynskey, M., & Degenhardt, L. (1998b). *The prevalence in the past year of substance use and ICD-10 substance use disorders in Australian adults: Findings from the national survey of mental health and well-being* (Technical Report 63). Sydney, Australia: National Drug and Alcohol Research Centre, UNSW.

Hando, J., Topp, L., & Hall, W. (1997). Amphetamine-related harms and treatment preferences of regular amphetamine users in Sydney, Australia. *Drug and Alcohol Dependence*, *46* (1–2), 105–113.

Hawkins, J., Catalano, R., & Miller, J. (1992). Risk and protective factors for alcohol and other drug problems in adolescence and early adulthood: Implications for substance abuse prevention. *Psychological Bulletin*, *112*, 64–105.

Hayashida, M., Alterman, A.I., McLellan, A.T., O'Brien, C.P., Purtill, J.J., Volpicelli, J.R., Raphaelson, A.H., & Hall, C.P. (1989). Comparative effectiveness and costs of inpatient and outpatient detoxification of patients with mild-to-moderate alcohol withdrawal syndrome. *The New England Journal of Medicine*, *320*, 358–365.

Heath, A. (1995). Genetic influences on alcoholism risk: A review of adoption and twin studies. *Alcohol Health and Research World*, *19* (3), 166–171.

Heath, A., & Martin, N. (1993). Genetic models for the natural history of smoking: Evidence for a genetic influence on smoking persistence. *Addictive Behaviors*, *18*, 19–34.

Heath, D.B. (2000). *Drinking occasions: Comparative perspectives on alcohol and culture*. Ann Arbor, MI: Sheridan Books.

Heather, N. (1992). Disulfirum treatment for alcoholism: Deserves re-evaluation. *British Medical Journal*, *1*, 471–472.

Heather, N. (1995a). Brief intervention strategies. In R.K. Hester & W.R. Miller (Eds.), *Handbook of alcoholism treatment approaches: Effective alternatives* (2nd ed., pp. 105–122). Boston, USA: Allyn & Bacon Inc.

Heather, N. (1995b). Interpreting the evidence on brief interventions for excessive drinkers: The need for caution. *Alcohol and Alcoholism*, *30* (3), 287–296.

Heather, N., & Greeley, J. (1990). Cue exposure in the treatment of drug dependence: The potential of a new method for preventing relapse. *Drug and Alcohol Review*, *9*, 155–168.

Heather, N., & Robertson, I. (1983). *Controlled drinking*. London: Methuen.

Heather, N., & Tebbutt, J. (1989). *The effectiveness of treatment for drug and alcohol problems: An overview*. Canberra: Commonwealth Department of Community Services and Health. National Campaign Against Drug Abuse (NCADA).

Heatherton, T., Kozlowski, L., Frecker, R., & Fagerström, K. (1991). The Fagerström test for nicotine dependence: A revision of the Fagerström Tolerance Questionnaire. *British Journal of Addiction*, *86*, 1119–1127.

Hebert, S. (1999). Bupropion (Zyban®, sustained-release): Reported adverse reactions. *Canadian Medical Association Journal, 160* (7), 1050–1051.

Helzer, J.E., Burnam, A., & McEvoy, L.T. (1991). Alcohol abuse and dependence. In L.N. Robins & D.A. Regier (Eds.), *Psychiatric disorders in America: The Epidemiologic Catchment Area study* (pp. 81–115). New York: The Free Press.

Henningfield, J., & Keenan, R. (1993). Nicotine delivery kinetics and abuse liability. *Journal of Consulting and Clinical Psychology, 61*, 7443–7450.

Henningfield, J., Lakshmi, G., & Shiffman, S. (1998). Tobacco dependence: Fundamental concepts and recent advances. *Current Opinion in Psychiatry, 11* (3), 259–263.

Henry, B., Feehan, M., McGee, R., Stanton, W., Moffitt, T., & Silva, P. (1993). The importance of conduct problems and depressive symptoms in predicting adolescent substance use. *Journal of Abnormal Child Psychology, 21*, 469–480.

Herrnstein, R., & Prelec, D. (1992). A theory of addiction. In G. Loewenstein & J. Elster (Eds.), *Choice over time* (pp. 331–360). New York: The Russell Sage Foundation.

Hester, R.K. (1995). What works? A methodological analysis of the alcohol treatment outcome literature. In R.K. Hester & W.R. Miller (Eds.), *Handbook of alcoholism treatment approaches: Effective alternatives* (pp. 12–44). Boston, USA: Allyn & Bacon.

Hester, R.K., & Delaney, H.D. (1997). Behavioral self-control program for Windows: Results of a controlled clinical trial. *Journal of Consulting and Clinical Psychology, 65* (4), 686–693.

Hoefler, M., Lieb, R., Perkonigg, A., Schuster, P., Sonntag, H., & Wittchen, H.-U. (1999). Covariates of cannabis use progression in a representative population sample of adolescents: A prospective examination of vulnerability and risk factors. *Addiction, 94* (11), 1679–1694.

Holder, H.D., & Blose, J.O. (1986). Alcoholism treatment and total health care utilization and costs: A four year longitudinal analysis of federal employees. *Journal of the American Medical Association, 256*, 1456–1460.

Holder, H.D., & Schachman, R.H. (1987). Estimating health care savings associated with alcoholism treatment. *Alcoholism: Clinical and experimental research, 11*, 66–73.

Homel, R. (1989). Crime on the roads: Drinking and driving. In J. Vernon (Ed.), *Alcohol and crime*. Canberra: Australian Institute of Criminology.

Hubbard, R.L., Craddock, S.G., Flynn, P.M., Anderson, J., & Etheridge, R.M. (1997). Overview of 1-year follow-up outcomes in the Drug Abuse Treatment Outcome Study (DATOS). *Psychology of Addictive Behaviors, 11* (4), 261–278.

Hughes, J.R., Stead, L.F., & Lancaster, T. (1999). Anxioloytics and antidepressants for smoking cessation (Cochrane review), *The Cochrane library* (Vol. 2). Oxford: Update Software.

Hurt, R.D., Sachs, D.P.L., Glover, E.D., Offord, K.P., Johnston, J.A., Dale, L.C., Khayrallah, M.A., Schroeder, D.R., Glover, P.N., Sullivan, C.R., Croghan, I.T., & Sullivan, P.M. (1997). A comparison of sustained-release bupropion and placebo for smoking cessation. *New England Journal of Medicine, 337* (17), 1195–1202.

Institute of Medicine. (1996). *Pathways of addiction*. Washington: National Academy Press.

Jarvis, T., Tebbit, J., & Mattick, R. (1994). *Treatment approaches for alcohol and drug dependence*. Sydney: Wiley.

Johnson, R.E., Jaffe, J.H., & Fudala, P.J. (1992). A controlled trial of buprenorphine treatment for opiod dependence. *Journal of the American Medical Association, 267*, 2750–2755.

Jorenby, D.E., Leischow, S.J., Nides, M.A., Rennard, S.I., Johnston, J.A., Hughes,

A.R., Smith, S.S., Muramoto, M.L., Daughton, D.M., Doan, K., Fiore, M.C., & Baker, T.B. (1999). A controlled trial of sustained-release bupropion, a nicotine patch, or both for smoking cessation. *New England Journal of Medicine*, 340 (9), 685–691.

Kamieniecki, G., Vincent, N., Allsop, S., & Lintzeris, N. (1998). *Models of intervention and care for psychostimulant users* (Monograph Series No. 32). Canberra, ACT: National Centre for Education and Training on Addiction.

Kampman, K.M., Volpicelli, J.R., McGinnis, D.E., Alterman, A.I., Weinrieb, R.M., D'Angelo, L., & Epperson, L.E. (1998). Reliability and validity of the Cocaine Selective Severity Assessment. *Addictive Behaviors*, 23 (4), 449–461.

Kendler, K., Neale, M., Sullivan, P., Corey, L., Gardner, C., & Prescott, C. (1999a). A population-based twin study in women of smoking initiation and nicotine dependence. *Psychological Medicine*, 29 (2), 299–308.

Kendler, K.S. (1999). Preparing for gene discovery: A further agenda for psychiatry. *Archives of General Psychiatry*, 56 (6), 554–555.

Kendler, K.S., Davis, C.G., & Kessler, R.C. (1997). The familial aggregation of common psychiatric and substance use disorders in the National Comorbidity Survey: A family history study. *British Journal of Psychiatry*, 170, 541–548.

Kendler, K.S., & Gardner Jr., C.O. (1998). Twin studies of adult psychiatric and substance dependence disorders: Are they biased by differences in the environmental experiences of monozygotic and dizygotic twins in childhood and adolescence? *Psychological Medicine*, 28 (3), 625–633.

Kendler, K.S., Heath, A.C., Neale, M.C., Kessler, R.C., & Eaves, L.J. (1992). A population-based twin study of alcoholism in women. *Journal of the American Medical Association*, 268 (14), 1877–1882.

Kendler, K.S., Karkowski, L.M., & Prescott, C.A. (1999b). Causal relationship between stressful life events and the onset of major depression. *American Journal of Psychiatry*, 156 (6), 837–841.

Kendler, K.S., Neale, M.C., Heath, A.C., Kessler, R.C., & Eaves, L.J. (1994). A twin-family study of alcoholism in women. *American Journal of Psychiatry*, 151 (5), 707–715.

Kendler, K.S., & Prescott, C.A. (1998a). Cannabis use, abuse, and dependence in a population-based sample of female twins. *American Journal of Psychiatry*, 155 (8), 1016–1022.

Kendler, K.S., & Prescott, C.A. (1998b). Cocaine use, abuse and dependence in a population-based sample of female twins. *British Journal of Psychiatry*, 173, 345–350.

Kidorf, M., Hollander, J.R., King, V.L., & Brooner, R.K. (1998). Increasing employment of opioid dependent outpatients: An intensive behavioural intervention. *Drug and Alcohol Dependence*, 50 (1), 73–80.

Kleber, H.D. (1998). Ultrarapid opiate detoxification. *Addiction*, 93 (11), 1629–1633.

Klee, H. (1992). A new target for behavioural research – amphetamine misuse. *British Journal of Addiction*, 87, 439–446.

Koob, G., Caine, S., Parsons, L., Markou, A., & Weiss, F. (1997). Opponent process model and psychostimulant addiction. *Pharmacology, Biochemistry and Behavior*, 57 (3), 513–521.

Koob, G.F., & LeMoal, M. (1997). Drug abuse: Hedonic homeostatic dysregulation. *Science*, 278, 52–58.

Kosten, T. (1990). Current pharmacotherapies for opiate dependence. *Psychopharmacology Bulletin*, 26, 69–74.

Krishnan-Sarin, S., Rosen, M., & O'Malley,

S. (1999). Preliminary evidence of an opioid component in nicotine dependence. *Archives of General Psychiatry, 56,* 663–668.

Laforge, R., Velicer, W., Richmond, R., & Owen, N. (1999). Stage distributions for five health behaviors in the United States and Australia. *Preventive Medicine, 28,* 61–74.

Lancaster, T., & Stead, L.F. (2000). Individual behavioural counselling for smoking cessation. *Cochrane Database of Systematic Reviews, 2.*

Lerman, C., Caporaso, N., Audrain, J., Main, D., Bowman, E., Lockshin, B., Boyd, N., & Shields, P. (1999). Evidence suggesting the role of specific genetic factors in cigarette smoking. *Health Psychology, 18* (1), 14–20.

Ling, W., Charuvastra, C., Kaim, S.C., & Klett, C.J. (1976). Methadyl acetate and methadone as maintenance treatments for heroin addicts. *Archives of General Psychiatry, 33* (6), 709–720.

Ling, W., & Wesson, D.R. (1984). Naltrexone treatment for addicted health-care professionals: A collaborative private practice experience. *Journal of Clinical Psychiatry, 45* (9 Pt. 2), 46–48.

Loeber, R., Southamer-Lober, M., & White, H. (1999). Developmental aspects of delinquency and internalising problems and their association with persistent juvenile substance use between ages 7 and 18. *Journal of Clinical Child Psychology, 28,* 322–332.

Loxley, W., Carruthers, J., & Bevan, J. (1995). *In the same vein.* Perth: National Centre for Research into the Prevention of Drug Abuse, Curtin University of Technology.

Lynskey, M., & Hall, W. (1998a). *Cannabis use among Australian youth* (NDARC Technical Report No. 66). Sydney, Australia: National Drug and Alcohol Research Centre.

Lynskey, M., & Hall, W. (1998b). *Jurisdictional trends in opioid overdose deaths, 1988–1996* (Technical Report No. 54). Sydney: National Drug and Alcohol Research Centre.

Lynskey, M., & Hall, W. (2000). *The educational consequences of early cannabis use among adolescents.* Sydney: NSW Department of Education and Training.

Madden, P.A.F., Bucholz, K.K., Dinwiddie, S.H., Slutske, W.S., Bierut, L.J., Statham, D.J., Dunne, M.P., Martin, N.G., & Heath, A.C. (1997). Nicotine withdrawal in women. *Addiction, 92* (7), 889–902.

Majewska, M.D. (1996). Cocaine addiction as a neurological disorder: Implications for treatment. *NIDA Research Monograph, 163,* 1–26.

Manschreck, T.C. (1993). The treatment of cocaine abuse. *Psychiatric Quarterly, 64* (2), 183–197.

Markou, A., Kosten, T., & Koob, G. (1998). Neurobiological similarities in depression and drug dependence: A self-medication hypothesis. *Neuropsychopharmacology, 18,* 135–174.

Marlatt, G.A., & Gordon, J.R. (Eds.) (1985). *Relapse prevention: Maintenance strategies in the treatment of addictive behaviors.* New York: Guilford Press.

Marlatt, G.A., & VandenBos, G.R. (1997). *Addictive behaviors: Readings on etiology, prevention, and treatment.* Washington, DC: American Psychological Association.

Mattick, R.P., & Baillie, A. (1992). *An outline for approaches to smoking cessation: Quality assurance in the treatment of a drug dependence project.* Canberra, Australia: Australian Government Publishing Service.

Mattick, R.P., & Darke, S. (1995). Drug replacement treatments: Is amphetamine substitution a horse of a different colour? *Drug and Alcohol Review, 14* (4), 389–394.

Mattick, R.P., & Hall, W. (1993). *A treatment outline for approaches to opioid dependence*. Sydney: National Drug and Alcohol Research Centre (NDARC).

Mattick, R.P., & Hall, W. (1996). Are detoxification programs effective? *Lancet, 347* (1), 97–100.

Mattick, R.P., & Jarvis, T. (Eds.) (1993). *An outline for the management of alcohol problems: Quality assurance project.* Canberra: Australian Government Publishing Service.

Mayfield, D., McLeod, G., & Hall, P. (1974). The CAGE questionnaire: Validation of a new alcohol screening instrument. *American Journal of Psychiatry, 131*, 1121–1123.

Mayo-Smith, M.F. (1997). Pharmacological management of alcohol withdrawal: A meta-analysis and evidence-based practice guideline. American Society of Addiction Medicine Working Group on Pharmacological Management of Alcohol Withdrawal. *Journal of the American Medical Association, 278* (2), 144–151.

McAfee, T., & France, E. (1998). Sustained-release bupropion for smoking cessation. *New England Journal of Medicine, 338* (9), 619–620.

McKetin, R., & Mattick, R.P. (1997). Attention and memory in illicit amphetamine users. *Drug and Alcohol Dependence, 48*, 235–242.

McKetin, R., & Mattick, R.P. (1998). Attention and memory in illicit amphetamine users: Comparison with non-drug using controls. *Drug and Alcohol Dependence, 50*, 181–184.

Meltzer, H., Gill, B., Petticrew, M., & Hinds, K. (1995). *The prevalence of psychiatric morbidity among adults living in private households.* (Surveys of Psychiatric Morbidity in Great Britain 1.) London: OPCS Social Surveys Division, HMSO.

Mendelson, C., & Richmond, R. (1994). The nicotine patch: Guidelines for practical use. *Modern Medicine*, 104–112.

Merikangas, K. (1990). The genetic epidemiology of alcoholism. *Psychological Medicine, 20*, 11–22.

Merikangas, K.R., Stevens, D.E., Fenton, B., Stolar, M., O'Malley, S., Woods, S.W., & Risch, N. (1998). Co-morbidity and familial aggregation of alcoholism and anxiety disorders. *Psychological Medicine, 28* (4), 773–788.

Miller, N.S., & Gold, M.S. (1998). Management of withdrawal syndromes and relapse prevention in drug and alcohol dependence. *American Family Physician, 58* (1), 139–146.

Miller, W., & Brown, J. (1991). Self-regulation as a conceptual basis for the prevention and treatment of addictive behaviours. In N. Heather, W. Miller, & J. Greeley (Eds.), *Self-control and the addictive behaviours* (pp. 3–79). Sydney: Maxwell Macmillan Publishing Australia.

Miller, W.R. (1980). The addictive behaviors. In W.R. Miller (Ed.), *The addictive behaviors* (pp. 3–7). Oxford: Pergamon Press.

Miller, W.R., Brown, J.M., Simpson, T.L., Handmaker, N.S., Bien, T.H., Luckie, L.F., Montgomery, H.A., Hester, R.K., & Tonigan, J.S. (1995). What works? A methodological analysis of the alcohol treatment outcome literature. In R.K. Hester & W.R. Miller (Eds.), *Handbook of alcoholism treatment approaches: Effective alternatives* (pp. 12–44). Boston, USA: Allyn & Bacon.

Miller, W.R., & Marlatt, G.A. (1984). *Comprehensive Drinker Profile (CDP).* Odessa, FL: Psychological Assessment Resources.

Monti, P.M., Rosenow, D.J., Colby, S.M., & Abrams, D.B. (1995). Coping and social skills training. In R.K. Hester & W.R. Miller (Eds.), *Handbook of alcoholism treatment approaches: Effective alternatives* (2nd ed.). Boston, USA: Allyn & Bacon.

Murray, C., & Lopez, A. (1996). *The global burden of disease: A comprehensive assessment of mortality and disability for* diseases, injuries, and risk factors in 1990 and projected to 2020. Cambridge, MA: Harvard University School of Public Health on behalf of the World Health Organization and The World Bank.

National Drug and Alcohol Research Centre. (1999). *Drugs: Just the facts* (2nd ed.). Sydney: NSW Department of Education and Training.

Newcomb, M.D., Maddahian, E., & Bentler, P.M. (1986). Risk factors for drug use among adolescents: Concurrent and longitudinal analyses. *American Journal of Public Health, 76* (5), 525–531.

Novello, A. (1990). US Surgeon General's report on the health benefits of smoking cessation. *Public Health Reports, 105,* 545–548.

Nutt, D. (1997). The neurochemistry of addiction. *Human Psychopharmacology, 12,* s53–s58.

Oliveto, A., & Kosten, T. (1997). Buprenorphine. In S. Stine & T. Kosten (Eds.), *New treatments for opioid dependence* (pp. 254–267). New York: Guilford Press.

Pears, D. (1984). *Motivated irrationality.* Oxford: Oxford University Press.

Pedersen, C.M. (1986). Hospital admissions from a non-medical alcohol detoxification unit. *Australian Drug and Alcohol Review, 5,* 133–137.

Platt, J.J. (1997). *Cocaine addiction: Theory, research, and treatment.* Cambridge, Massachusetts: Harvard University Press.

Pomerleau, O., & Kardia, S. (1999). Introduction to the featured section: Genetic research on smoking. *Health Psychology, 18* (1), 3–6.

Pomerleau, O., & Pomerleau, C. (1988). *Nicotine replacement – a critical evaluation.* New York: Alan R. Liss Publishers.

Prescott, C.A., & Kendler, K.S. (1999). Genetic and environmental contributions to alcohol abuse and dependence in a population-based sample of male twins. *American Journal of Psychiatry, 156* (1), 34–40.

Prescott, C.A., Neale, M.C., Corey, L.A., & Kendler, K.S. (1997). Predictors of problem drinking and alcohol dependence in a population-based sample of female twins. *Journal of Studies on Alcohol, 58* (2), 167–181.

Prochaska, J.O., & DiClemente, C.C. (1986). Toward a comprehensive model of change. In W.R. Miller & N. Heather (Eds.), *Treating addictive behaviors* (2nd ed., pp. 3–27). New York and London: Plenum Press.

Project MATCH Research Group. (1997). Matching alcoholism treatments to client heterogeneity: Project MATCH posttreatment drinking outcomes. *Journal of Studies on Alcohol, 58,* 7–29.

Proudfoot, H., & Teesson, M. (2000). *Investing in drug and alcohol treatment* (Technical Report No. 91). Sydney: National Drug and Alcohol Research Centre, UNSW.

Raistrick, D., Dunbar, G., & Davidson, R. (1983). Development of a questionnaire to measure alcohol dependence. *British Journal of Addiction, 78,* 89–95.

Rawson, R.A., & Tennant, F.S. (1984). Five year follow-up of opiate addicts with naltrexone and behaviour therapy. In L.S. Harris (Ed.), *NIDA Research Monograph No. 49 – problems of drug dependence, Proceedings of the 45th Annual Scientific Meeting, The Committee on Problems of Drug Dependence.* Rockville, MD: US Department of Health and Human Services.

Rees, V., Copeland, J., & Swift, W. (1998). *Manual for brief cognitive behavioural therapy for cannabis dependence* (Technical Report No. 65). Sydney, Australia: National Drug and Alcohol Research Centre, UNSW.

Regier, D.A., Farmer, M.E., Rae, D.S., Locke, B.Z., Keith, S.J., Judd, L.L., & Goodwin, F.K. (1990). Comorbidity of mental disorders with alcohol and other drug abuse: Results from the Epidemiologic Catchment Area (ECA) study. *Journal of the American Medical Association, 264*, 2511–2518.

Regier, D.A., Narrow, W.E., Rae, D.S., Manderscheid, R.W., Locke, B., & Goodwin, F.K. (1993). The de facto US mental and addictive disorders service system: Epidemiologic Catchment Area prospective study 1-year prevalence rates of disorders and services. *Archives of General Psychiatry, 50*, 85–94.

Richmond, R., Kehoe, L., & Neto, A.C. (1997). Effectiveness of a 24-hour transdermal nicotine patch in conjunction with a cognitive behavioural programme: One year outcome. *Addiction, 92* (2), 27–31.

Robins, L. (1978). Sturdy childhood predictors of adult anti-social behavior: Replications from longitudinal studies. *Psychological Medicine, 8*, 611–622.

Robins, L.N., & Regier, D.A. (Eds.). (1991). *Psychiatric disorders in America: The Epidemiologic Catchment Area study.* New York: The Free Press.

Rollnick, S., Butler, C., & Hodgson, R. (1997). Brief alcohol intervention in medical settings. *Addiction Research, 5* (4), 331–342.

Romach, M., Glue, P., Kampman, K., Kaplan, H., Somer, G., Poole, S., Clarke, L., Coffin, V., Cornish, J., O'Brien, C., & Sellers, E. (1999). Attentuation of the euphoric effects of cocaine by the dopamine D1/D5 antagonist Ecopipam (SCH 39166). *Archives of General Psychiatry, 56*, 1101–1106.

Roth, A., Hogan, I., & Farren, C. (1997). Naltrexone plus group therapy for the treatment of opiate-abusing health-care professionals. *Journal of Substance Abuse Treatment, 14* (1), 19–22.

Royal College of Physicians of London. (1992). *Smoking and the young.* London: Royal College of Physicians of London.

Russell, M., & Bigler, L. (1979). Screening for alcohol-related problems in an outpatient obstetric-gynecologic clinic. *American Journal of Obstetrics and Gynaecology, 134*, 4–12.

Sabol, S., Nelson, M., Fisher, C., Gunzerath, L., Brody, C., Hu, S., Sirota, L., Marcus, S., Greenberg, B., Lucas, F., Benjamin, J., Murphy, D., & Hamer, D. (1999). A genetic association for cigarette smoking behavior. *Health Psychology, 18* (1), 7–13.

Saunders, B., & Allsop, S. (1991). Incentives and restraints: Clinical research into problem drug use and self-control. In N. Heather, W. Miller, & J. Greeley (Eds.), *Self-control and the addictive behaviours* (pp. 283–303). Sydney: Maxwell Macmillan.

Saunders, J.B., Aasland, O.G., Babor, T.F., delaFuente, J.R., & Grant, M. (1993). Development of the Alcohol Use Disorders Identification Test (AUDIT): WHO collaborative project on early detection of persons with harmful alcohol consumption – II. *Addiction, 88*, 791–804.

Schuckit, M. (1999). New findings in the genetics of alcoholism. *Journal of the American Medical Association, 281*, 1875–1876.

Schuckit, M.A. (1994). The treatment of stimulant dependence. *Addiction, 89*, 1559–1563.

Schuckit, M.A. (1996). Recent developments in the pharmacotherapy of alcohol dependence. *Journal of Consulting and Clinical Psychology, 64* (4), 669–676.

Selzer, M.L. (1971). The Michigan alcoholism screening test: The quest for a new diagnostic instrument. *American Journal of Psychiatry, 127*, 85–94.

Shiffman, S., & Jarvik, M. (1976). Smoking withdrawal symptoms in two weeks of abstinence. *Psychopharmacology, 50*, 35–39.

Sidney, S., Beck, J., & Tekawa, I. (1997).

Marijuana use and mortality. *American Journal of Public Health, 87,* 585–590.

Silagy, C., Mant, D., Fowler, G., & Lodge, M. (1994). Meta-analysis on efficacy of nicotine replacement therapies in smoking cessation. *Lancet, 343,* 139–142.

Simpson, D., & Sells, S. (1982). Effectiveness of treatment for drug abuse: An overview of the DARP research program. *Advances in Alcohol and Substance Abuse, 2,* 7–29.

Sitharthan, T., & Kavanagh, D.J. (1991). Role of self efficacy in predicting outcomes for a programme for controlled drinking. *Drug and Alcohol Dependence, 27* (1), 87–94.

Sitharthan, T., Kavanagh, D.J., & Sayer, G. (1996). Moderating drinking by correspondence: An evaluation of a new method of intervention. *Addiction, 91* (3), 345–355.

Skinner, H.A., & Horn, J.L. (1984). *Alcohol Dependence Scale (ADS): Users' guide.* Toronto: ARF.

Skog, O.-J. (1999). Rationality, irrationality and addiction – notes on Becker and Murphy's theory of addiction. In J. Elster & O.-J. Skog (Eds.), *Getting hooked: Rationality and addiction.* Cambridge: Cambridge University Press.

Smelson, D.A., McGee Caulfield, E., Bergstein, P., & Engelhart, C. (1999). Initial validation of the Voris Cocaine Craving Scale: A preliminary report. *Journal of Clinical Psychology, 55* (1), 135–139.

Smith, D.E., & Gay, G.R. (1972). *"It's so good, don't even try it once": Heroin in perspective.* Englewood Cliffs, NJ: Prentice-Hall.

Smith, J.E., Meyers, R.J., & Delaney, H.D. (1998). The community reinforcement approach with homeless alcohol-dependent individuals. *Journal of Consulting and Clinical Psychology, 66* (3), 541–548.

Smith, J.W., Schmeling, G., & Knowles,

P.L. (1988). A marijuana cessation clinical trial utilising THC-free marijuana, aversion therapy, and self-management counselling. *Journal of Substance Abuse Treatment, 5,* 89–98.

Sobell, M.B., & Sobell, L.C. (1995a). Controlled drinking after 25 years: How important was the great debate? *Addiction, 90* (9), 1149–1153.

Sobell, M.B., & Sobell, L.C. (1995b). Controlled drinking after 25 years: How important was the great debate? [editorial]. *Addiction, 90* (9), 1149–1153; discussion 1157–1177.

Spealman, R. (1990). Antagonism of the behavioral effects of cocaine by selective dopamine receptor blockers. *Psychopharmacology, 101,* 142–145.

Spealman, R., Bargman, J., Madras, B., & Melia, K. (1991). Discriminative stimulus effects of cocaine in squirrel monkeys: Involvement of dopamine receptor subtypes. *Journal of Pharmacology and Experimental Therapy, 258,* 945–953.

Stahl, S. (1996) *Essential Psychopharmacology.* Cambridge: Cambridge University Press.

Stead, L.F., & Lancaster, T. (2000). Group behaviour therapy programmes for smoking cessation. *Cochrane Database of Systematic Reviews, 2.*

Stephens, R., Roffman, R., & Simpson, E. (1994a). Treating adult marijuana dependence: A test of the relapse prevention model. *Journal of Consulting and Clinical Psychology, 62* (1), 92–99.

Stephens, R.S., Roffman, R.A., & Simpson, E.E. (1994b). Treating adult marijuana dependence: A test of the relapse prevention model. *Journal of Consulting and Clinical Psychology, 62* (1), 92–99.

Stine, S., & Kosten, T. (Eds.) (1997). *Treatments for opioid dependence.* New York: Guilford Press.

Stitzer, M.L., & DeWit, H. (1998). Abuse liability of nicotine. In N.L. Benowitz (Ed.), *Nicotine safety and toxicity* (pp.

119–131). New York: Oxford University Press.

Stockwell, T., Bolt, L., Milner, I., Pugh, P., & Young, I. (1990). Home detoxification for problem drinkers: Acceptability to clients, relatives, general practitioners and outcome after 60 days. *British Journal of Addiction*, 85, 61–70.

Stockwell, T., Murphy, D., & Hodgson, R. (1983). The Severity of Alcohol Dependence Questionnaire: Its use, reliability and validity. *British Journal of Addiction*, 78, 145–155.

Stockwell, T., Sitharthan, T., McGrath, D., & Lang, E. (1994). The measurement of alcohol dependence and impaired control in community samples. *Addiction*, 89, 167–174.

Sutherland, G., Edwards, G., Taylor, C., Phillips, G., Gossop, M., & Brady, R. (1986). The measurement of opiate dependence. *British Journal of Addiction*, 81, 485–494.

Swift, W., Copeland, J., & Hall, W. (1997). *Cannabis dependence among long-term users in Sydney, Australia* (Technical Report No. 47). Sydney, Australia: National Drug and Alcohol Research Centre.

Swift, W., Copeland, J., & Hall, W. (1998). Choosing a diagnostic cut-off for cannabis dependence. *Addiction*, 93 (11), 1681–1692.

Tagliaro, F., De Battisti, Z., Smith, F.P., & Marigo, M. (1998). Death from heroin overdose: Findings from hair analysis. *Lancet*, 351 (9120), 1923–1935.

Tarter, R., & Mezzich, A. (1992). Ontogeny of substance abuse: Perspectives and findings. In M. Glantz & R. Pickens (Eds.), *Vulnerability to drug abuse* (pp. 75–98). Washington, DC: American Psychological Association.

Teesson, M., Hall, W., Lynskey, M., & Degenhardt, L. (2000a). Alcohol and drug use disorders in Australia: Implications of the National Survey of Mental Health and Wellbeing.

Australian and New Zealand Journal of Psychiatry, 34, 206–213.

Teesson, M., Hodder, T., & Buhrich, N. (2000b). Substance use disorders among homeless people in inner Sydney. *Social Psychiatry and Psychiatric Epidemiology*, 35, 451–456.

Teesson, M., Lynskey, M., Manor, B., & Baillie, A. (submitted). Psychometric properties of DSM-IV cannabis use disorders. *Psychological Medicine*.

Thun, M.J., Peto, R., Lopez, A.D., et al. (1997). Alcohol consumption and mortality among middle-aged and elderly US adults. *New England Journal of Medicine*, 337, 1704–1714.

Tonigan, J.S., Toscova, R., & Miller, W.R. (1996). Meta-analysis of the literature on Alcoholics Anonymous: Sample and study characteristics. *Journal of Studies on Alcohol*, 57, 65–72.

Torrens, M., San, L., Peri, J.M., & Olle, J.M. (1991). Cocaine abuse among heroin addicts in Spain. *Drug and Alcohol Dependence*, 27, 29–34.

Torres, M., Mattick, R., Chen, R., & Baillie, A. (1995). *Clients of treatment service agencies*. Canberra: Commonwealth Department of Health and Aged Care.

True, W., Xian, H., Scherrer, J., Madden, P., Bucholz, K., Heath, A., Eisen, S., Lyons, M., Goldberg, J., & Tsuang, M. (1999). Common genentic vulnerability for nicotine and alcohol dependence. *Archives of General Psychiatry*, 56, 655–661.

Tsuang, M., Lyons, M., Eisen, S., Goldberg, J., True, W., Lin, N., Meyer, J., Toomey, R., Faraone, S., & Eaves, L. (1996). Genetic influences on DSM-III-R drug abuse and dependence: A study of 3,372 twin pairs. *American Journal of Medical Genetics (Neuropsychiatric Genetics)*, 67, 473–477.

Tsuang, M.T., Lyons, M.J., Meyer, J.M., Doyle, T., Eisen, S.A., Goldberg, J., True, W., Lin, N., Toomey, R., & Eaves,

L. (1998). Co-occurrence of abuse of different drugs in men: The role of drug-specific and shared vulnerabilities [see comments]. *Archives of General Psychiatry, 55* (11), 967–972.

Tutton, C.S., & Crayton, J.W. (1993). Current pharmacotherapies for cocaine abuse: A review. *Journal of Addictive Diseases, 12* (2), 109–127.

Uchtenhagen-Gutzwiller, F., & Dobler-Mikola, A. (1997). *Programme for a medical prescription of narcotics.* Zurich: Zurich Institute for Social and Preventive Medicine, University of Zurich.

US Department of Health Education and Welfare. (1964). *The health consequences of smoking.* Washington, DC: Government Printing Office.

US Department of Health Education and Welfare. (1971). *The health consequences of smoking.* Washington, DC: Government Printing Office.

US Department of Health Education and Welfare. (1979). *The health consequences of smoking.* Washington, DC: Government Printing Office.

US Department of Health Education and Welfare. (1984). *The health consequences of smoking.* Washington, DC: Government Printing Office.

US Department of Health Education and Welfare. (1988). *The health consequences of smoking.* Washington, DC: Government Printing Office.

US Office of National Drug Control Policy. (1998). *Pulse check.* Washington, DC: Office of National Drug Control Policy.

US Surgeon General. (1982). *The health consequences of smoking. Cancer.* Rockville: US Department of Health and Human Services.

US Surgeon General. (1986). *The health consequences of involuntary smoking.* Rockville: US Department of Health and Human Services.

Volpicelli, J.R. (1992). Naltrexone in the treatment of alcohol dependence. *Archives of General Psychiatry, 49,* 876–880.

Walsh, D., & Hingson, R. (1987). Epidemiology and alcohol policy. In S. Levine & A. Lilienfeld (Eds.), *Epidemiology and public policy* (pp. 265–291). New York: Tavistock.

Ward, J., Mattick, R.P., & Hall, W. (Eds.). (1998). *Methadone maintenance treatment and other opioid replacement therapies.* Amsterdam: OPA.

Washton, A.M., Gold, M.S., & Pottash, A.C. (1984). Naltrexone in addicted physicians and business executives. *NIDA Research Monograph, 55,* 185–190.

Welsh, I. (1993) *Trainspotting.* London: Random House.

West, R. (1989). The psychological basis of addiction. *International Review of Psychiatry, 1,* 71–80.

White, A.R., Rampes, H., & Ernst, E. (2000). Acupuncture for smoking cessation. *Cochrane Database of Systematic Reviews, 2.*

Whitworth, A.B., Fischer, F., Lesch, O.M., Nimmerrichter, A., Oberbauer, H., Platz, T., Potgieter, A., Walter, H., & Fleischhacker, W.W. (1996). Comparison of acamprosate and placebo in long-term treatment of alcohol dependence [see comments]. *Lancet, 347* (9013), 1438–1442.

WHO Brief Intervention Study Group. (1996a). A cross-national trial of brief interventions with heavy drinkers. *American Journal of Public Health, 86* (7), 948–955.

WHO Brief Intervention Study Group. (1996b). A cross-national trial of brief interventions with heavy drinkers. WHO Brief Intervention Study Group. *American Journal of Public Health, 86* (7), 948–955.

Wilk, A.I., Jensen, N.M., & Havighurst, T.C. (1997). Meta-analysis of randomized control trials addressing brief interventions in heavy alcohol drinkers. *Journal of General Internal Medicine, 12* (5), 274–283.

Williams, B.T.R., & Drummond, D.C. (1994). The Alcohol Problems Questionnaire: Reliability and validity. *Drug and Alcohol Dependence, 35* (3), 239–243.

Williams, P. (1998). *Progress of the National Drug Strategy: Key national indicators.* Canberra: Australian Government Publishing Service.

Wise, R.A. (1996). Neurobiology of addiction. *Current Opinion in Neurobiology, 6* (2), 243–251.

World Health Organization. (1993). *The ICD-10 Classification of Mental and Behavioral Disorders.* Geneva, Switzerland: World Health Organization.

Zador, D., Sunjic, S., & Darke, S. (1996). Heroin-related deaths in New South Wales, 1992: Toxicological findings and circumstances [see comments]. *Medical Journal of Australia, 164* (4), 204–207.

Zweben, J.E., & O'Connell, K. (1992). Strategies for breaking marijuana dependence. *Journal of Psychoactive Drugs, 24,* 165–171.

Further reading

Edwards, G., Marshall, E.J., & Cook, C.C. (1997). *The treatment of drinking problems: A guide for the helping professions* (3rd ed.). New York: Cambridge University Press.

Hester R.K., & Miller, W.R. (Eds.) (1995). *Handbook of alcoholism treatment approaches: Effective alternatives*. Boston, USA: Allyn & Bacon.

Jarvis, T., Tebbit, J., & Mattick, R. (1994). *Treatment approaches for alcohol and drug dependence*. Sydney: Wiley.

Marlatt, G.A., & Gordon, J.R. (Eds.) (1985). *Relapse prevention. Maintenance strategies in the treatment of addictive behaviors.* New York: Guilford Press.

Teesson, M. (2000). Substance use disorders. In *Management of mental disorders* (3rd ed.). World Health Organization Collaborating Centre for Mental Health and Substance Abuse, Darlinghurst, NSW, Australia, 2010.

Ward, J., Mattick, R.P., & Hall, W. (Eds.) (1998). *Methadone maintenance treatment and other opioid replacement therapies.* Amsterdam: OPA.

Author index

Note: page numbers in *italics* refer to authors referred to in tables or boxes

Subject index

Note: page numbers in *italics* refer to information presented in tables, page numbers in **bold** refer to diagrams.

psychosis: amphetamine 27, 101; cocaine-induced 28; drug-induced 25, 26, 27, 28, 101

psychosocial interventions 106

psychostimulants: effects of 5; sites of action *34–5*, *see also* amphetamines; cocaine

psychostimulant dependence 3, 101–4; assessment 102; cognitive behavioural therapy 103–4; detoxification 103; health risks 101; interventions 102–4; pharmacotherapy 102–3, 104

psychoticism 42–3

psychotropic drugs 2, *3, see also specific drugs*

public health interventions 53–5, 66

questionnaires: for assessment of alcohol use disorders 50–2, *51*, 53; for assessment of cannabis dependency 82; for assessment of opiate dependency 92; for assessment of psychostimulant dependency 102

rational choice theories of addiction 43–4

relapse: alcohol use disorders 61; cannabis dependency 86–9; identifying the causes of 87–8; opiate dependency 94; prevention 61, 86–9; triggers 73

'relapse prevention training' 86–9

respiratory diseases 24

SCL-90 53

SCQ-39 82

screening: for alcohol use disorders 50–2, *51*, 56, 66; for comorbidity 53

sedatives *3, see also specific drugs*

self-efficacy: alcohol use disorders 52; cannabis-dependency 82

self-help groups: for alcohol use disorders 58, 60, 63, 67; for opiate dependency 94–5

self-regulation 41–2

Severity of Alcohol Dependence Questionnaire (SADQ) 52

Severity of Dependence Scale (SDS) 82–3, 84, 92

Severity of Opiate Dependence Questionnaire 92

sexual behaviour, and amphetamine use 27, 101

sexually transmitted infections 27

Shiffman Tobacco Withdrawal Scale 70

Short Alcohol Dependence Data Questionnaire (SADDQ) 52

siblings 37, 45

sites of action, drugs 33–6, *34–5*

smoking *see* cannabis; nicotine; tobacco smoking

social skills training 63

sociocultural factors, and addiction 45–6

solvents *3*

speedballs 27–8

stimulants *see* psychostimulants

substance abuse: alcohol 13, 49, 50, 61; diagnosing 7–8; illicit drugs 9, 15

Switzerland 106

delta-9-tetrahydrocannabinol (Δ^9-THC) *34*, 35, 36, 79–80

theories of addiction 33–47; biological 36–40; biopsychosocial 47; contextual 44–6; neuroscientific 33–6, *34–5*, 46; overview 33; psychological 40–4, 46

Therapeutic Communities (TCs) 94–5

tobacco smoking 69; abstinence 72, 73; acupuncture 76; antidepressants as cessation aid 75–6; assessment of dependence 69–71, *71*, 77; aversive smoking 76–7; client history 70; comorbidity 71, 76; counselling for 72–3; disease burden 69; genetic vulnerability to addiction 38, 39; group counselling for 73; health consequences 22–3, **22**, **23**, 24, 69; hypnotherapy for 77; intervention guidelines 73, 77; interventions for 71–7; nicotine replacement therapy 74–5, 76; prevalence 18–19; quit plan formulation 72; relapse triggers 73; withdrawal 70, 73, *see also* nicotine